"Although there are still many mctrum disorders, one thing generally ag tion is important for more positive, long ers an in-depth analysis of the quest for earlier identification strategies and training techniques and represents a major contribution that many will find invaluable. The research review is thorough and presented in a way that scientists, practitioners, and parents will be able to appreciate and understand. Its combination of scientific integrity, clear descriptions, and jargon-free explanations is one way that this book stands out. Another is that the book reflects the author's conviction that the use of many visuals, including pictures, photographs, and figures, is the best way for readers to understand the issues related to early identification of autism spectrum disorders and to develop the necessary observational skills to be effective researchers and practitioners."

—*Gary B. Mesibov, Ph.D., Professor Emeritus, The University of North Carolina at Chapel Hill*

"Patricia O'Brien Towle offers a fresh, new look at the intricacies of identification of autism in children. Her approach is very worth reviewing and taking into consideration when making this vital diagnostic call. Read, remember, and reference!"

—*Susan J. Moreno, CEO and Founder, OASIS@MAAP, MAAP Services for Autism and Asperger Syndrome*

"This is a very readable, thoughtful book that will be helpful to both professionals and family members seeking information about young children with autism spectrum disorders. The book is unique in several ways: its extensive use of pictures to represent both the skills that are often delayed or missing in children with ASD and unusual behaviors that may be present, and also in the way new topics are introduced through asking the questions foremost on parents and others' minds about what autism is. Dr. Towle's book makes a valuable contribution to our understanding of autism and our ability to communicate this understanding to the people for whom it matters most."

—*Catherine Lord, Ph.D., Director of the Center for Autism and the Developing Brain, a collaborative effort between New York Presbyterian Hospital, Weill Cornell Medical College and Columbia University Medical College in Partnership with New York Collaborates for Autism, and Professor of Psychology in Psychiatry at Weill Cornell Medical College*

The Early Identification *of* Autism Spectrum Disorders

A Visual Guide

Patricia O'Brien Towle

Jessica Kingsley *Publishers*
London and Philadelphia

First published in 2013
by Jessica Kingsley Publishers
116 Pentonville Road
London N1 9JB, UK
and
400 Market Street, Suite 400
Philadelphia, PA 19106, USA

www.jkp.com

Library of Congress Cataloging in Publication Data
A CIP catalog record for this book is available from the Library of Congress

British Library Cataloguing in Publication Data
A CIP catalogue record for this book is available from the British Library

ISBN 978 1 84905 329 7
eISBN 978 0 85700 683 7

Printed and bound in China

Contents

List of Figures

List of Tables

Introduction

This book grew out of many years of a certain combination of activities. As a child clinical psychologist, I have specialized in working with young children with developmental disabilities and their families. Yet because of the setting in which I practice, training others to work in this field is always an integral part of this clinical work. The training activities cover a broad range: direct supervision of doctoral-level psychology students, seminars and lectures to interdisciplinary groups of students and professionals, community-based inservices and continuing education, and local and national conferences. Thus, I have spent much of my professional life explaining the complex issues related to development and disability, teaching diagnostic assessment, and tying evaluation outcomes to intervention and the larger issues of the systems of care for individuals with developmental disabilities.

When I started using video to teach observation skills to apply to direct client contact, I quickly found that the learning curve of trainees increased dramatically with carefully chosen and narrated video clips. Through using video more and more in lectures and workshops, the power of the visual example became increasingly evident. Then, for a community training program, my team created a set of brochures using stills from the videos—and found that still pictures can also capture a moment and enhance verbal explanations immeasurably. Thus was born the idea for a larger work—a book that makes abundant use of figures, stills, and photographs that will prove effective in capturing the behaviors that represent the key issues in autism spectrum disorder in young children.

The goal of this book is to build observation skills in the service of early identification of autism spectrum disorder, as well as to increase understanding of the core behaviors that make up the profile of ASD. I strongly believe that a deep understanding of the communication, social, play, cognitive, and sensory information processing of young children with ASD and other disabilities must be the foundation for both evaluation and intervention. In the process of conducting formal assessments of these children, there are many choices of evaluation strategies and specific measurement instruments, but none is sufficient without extensive knowledge about the condition itself. In the same way, intervention can become formulaic and misguided unless that firm foundation exists of understanding the nature and development of the key behaviors—both those that make up a typical course of development and those that represent characteristics of autism.

It is hoped that this book will be useful for a broad variety of both professionals and professionals-in-training who work with children with disabilities and their families. This includes health and behavioral professionals such as psychologists, psychiatrists, pediatric neurologists, nurses, social workers, pediatricians, family doctors, developmental/ behavioral pediatricians, speech-language pathologists, special educators, and occupational and physical therapists. The information should be useful for both those who conduct assessments as well as those who are in a position to refer for evaluation and discuss concerns with parents about behaviors that may suggest a disability. As such, daycare and preschool teachers often find this information very useful as well.

This book would not have been possible without the generous contributions of many families who were willing to share their home movies with me. All the families who donated footage and consented to the use of images of their children and family members did so in the spirit of wishing to advance knowledge and help families access services and support. I am most grateful to them.

Dr. Towle is based at the Westchester Institute for Human Development (WIHD), a University Center for Excellence in Developmental Disabilities, in Valhalla, New York. WIHD's mission is to create better futures for people with disabilities, for vulnerable children, and for their families and caregivers. WIHD accomplishes its mission through professional education, innovative services and supports, community training and technical assistance, research, and information dissemination.

The Importance of Early Identification of Autism Spectrum Disorder

Public and professional awareness of autism and autism spectrum disorder (ASD) is now at an all-time high. Through the work of advocacy organizations and governmental public health campaigns, more children are being identified than ever before, and at earlier ages. Why is early identification such an important goal? And how early can children be diagnosed with ASD?

Why Early Intervention?

The major goal of detecting ASD at the earliest age is to enable the child and family to access intervention services as soon as possible. This conviction comes from several lines of reasoning. The first originates in our evolving understanding of the central nature of ASD. That is, since the best scientific evidence suggests that ASD is present from birth—in fact has a strong genetic component—then as symptoms unfold early in life, *this* is the time to address them. Not later, when patterns that interfere with learning are set, but when behaviors first show themselves and start to impact on how the child interacts with people and objects. The second line of reasoning stems from the knowledge that there are "critical periods" when the young brain is best primed to learn early language, social skills, and cognitive concepts. Early intervention endeavors to intervene during these optimal learning periods rather than try to recoup them later in life. Related to this idea is the central issue of brain *plasticity*—the demonstrated capacity of experiences during the time of early experience to shape neural connections and function.

The point of this approach is to attempt to "unseat" the autism behaviors so that the child eventually has fewer, and perhaps even negligible, symptoms as time goes on. But another rationale acknowledges that this is not going to be possible for every child. As ASD presents itself on a continuum of severity and springs from a variety of etiologies, many children will be "on the spectrum" for life, regardless of aggressive intervention. However, in this case early intervention is still of utmost importance because it gives the child the best start possible; it can build and shape communication, social, cognitive, and practical skills so that the child develops optimally. Just like all growth issues (think of how early healthy eating builds body tissues and functioning for the healthy adolescent and eventually adult), each phase in development builds on an earlier one, and the more firm a foundation is built, the better things proceed. Here the goal is the highest level of independent functioning and community inclusion that the individual may be capable of.

A third line of reasoning rests on the firm belief, in the field of early intervention and developmental disabilities, that the family is as much the recipient of services as the child is. Child-focused interventions endeavor to build the child's ability to communicate, navigate the environment physically, play with toys, and learn many things from the adults, peers, and activities in his environment. Family involvement is crucial not only in order to help those child-focused efforts along, but also, as importantly, to build advocacy skills on the part of the caregivers. Advocacy skills are those that enable parents to make decisions about their child's needs, access resources, and navigate the health, disabilities, and educational systems. The younger the child is, the more inextricable are child- and parent-focused intervention efforts. Therefore, best practice early intervention services are conducted in partnership with caregivers, and are not considered complete unless family members continually increase in confidence, knowledge, and decision-making skills (Tomasello, Manning, & Dulmus, 2010).

Apart from these logical arguments, we look to scientific evidence to inform us about whether early intervention has a positive impact, and which types of interventions work the best. At this point it would be naïve to claim that there is abundant, irrefutable evidence on all fronts that early intervention "works." It is extremely difficult to carry out rigorous intervention research in the behavioral sciences given all the various factors at work (which children are included, what symptoms are targeted, which intervention strategy is used, how long it is administered, what setting, therapist or teacher skill, parent follow-through, and so on). Yet, slowly but surely, enough evidence has been amassed so

that professional clinical guidelines recommend early intervention that is interdisciplinary, frequent, and intense. The most published studies exist on behaviorally based interventions, because they originated from academic settings, but increasingly researchers are investigating a variety of strategies and even combinations of them.

How Early Can ASD Be Detected?

The age at which ASD can and should be detected and diagnosed has been a moving target. Up until relatively recently the conventional wisdom was to wait until three years of age before determining that a child had a significant, ongoing communication or intellectual disability. But, as early intervention became more emphasized, as more focus fell upon autism and ASD, and as better screening and assessment instruments were developed, there was great interest in achieving earlier diagnoses.

Researchers turned their focus to the same set of questions. Initially, understanding how children with ASD developed depended on the retrospective recollection of parents. An important breakthrough came with studies in the 1990s using home movies donated by parents of children who were diagnosed with ASD (Saint-Georges *et al.*, 2010). From these studies, it became obvious that even at 12 months of age a significant percentage of children showed signs of ASD. Then, from the early 2000s, prospective studies enrolled newborn siblings (of children with confirmed autism diagnosis) with the expectation that up to 35 percent will develop an ASD because of genetic influences. The "Baby Sibs" are studied intensively from birth using a variety of investigative methods—some laboratories focus on brain development, some on genetics, and some on early language and social development. By the time the younger siblings are 30 to 36 months old, ASD then can be diagnosed or ruled out, and a tremendous amount of longitudinal data on young children with and without ASD have been gathered (see Rogers, 2009).

These studies have found the same thing that clinicians skilled in early diagnostic assessment were finding—that the majority of children could be diagnosed by age 24 months. And "*by* age 24 months" means that some children can be diagnosed earlier as well—18 to 20 months is not too young for those with obvious symptoms (to the trained eye, of course). From a clinical viewpoint, there are children for whom the diagnosis is not so clear at 24 months, but these tend to be those for whom diagnosis may remain equivocal for an extended time. These children have milder manifestations and show both strengths that seem to rule out an ASD and features of ASD that are hard to ignore.

Both clinical and research efforts continue to push the ASD diagnosis age downward. Some of the behaviors being focused on are how children below 12 months and even younger scan faces and objects visually, how they move physically, and features of their vocalization repertoire. Screening questionnaires that parents fill out as early as age 12 months have yielded some success (Pierce *et al.*, 2011). It is particularly challenging, however, to detect a developmental disability when in fact the child is developing rapidly at the same time. Early human development is the result of several complex systems interacting with one another. See the next chapter for a more thorough discussion of these issues.

Although these efforts are ongoing, the goal of having children detected and started in early intervention well before three years of age has not been accomplished except in parts of developed countries where there is a high concentration of resources (Mandell, Novak, & Zubritsky, 2005). Such resources consist of a sufficient number of trained professionals, diagnostic centers, and early intervention providers. Awareness is an important commodity as well—awareness on the part of parents themselves, and childcare and nursery school providers, as well as on the part of primary healthcare providers so that autism is screened for during well-child visits. This visual guide is intended to contribute to the training and awareness that is essential to increase our success in caring for children with ASD.

CHAPTER 2

Sources of Variability in Autism Spectrum Disorder in Young Children

The ASD Symptom Profile

What symptoms come to mind when ASD is mentioned? The usual are lack of eye contact, hand-flapping, spinning and twirling, unusual play, social isolation, and atypical vocalizations. There are many lists of "red flags" available, but the diagnosis of ASD is not dependent on the presence of a list of behaviors. ASD diagnosis depends upon a *profile* of symptoms.

All children with ASD will show challenges across the profile of:

- social interaction

- communication

- play and interests, or "restricted and repetitive behaviors."

If a child does not have significant challenges in each and all of these areas, then he does not have ASD. In the evolving world of formal diagnostic criteria, social interaction and communication areas are merging into "social communication," but there are still symptoms that can be considered independently in the social versus the communication sphere. The third symptom domain, which is more formally known as "restricted, repetitive, and stereotyped behavior and interests," needs to be understood in the context of early play and object use in the case of very young children. Another symptom area involving atypical sensory processing has emerged as important in the profile as well. The subsequent chapters of this book will go into detail about the nature of these symptom domains and their component features.

Checklists that are offered in public health awareness campaigns or websites designed to offer information to the public may be useful in promoting general awareness of ASD, but they do not provide the framework that is needed to understand the complexity of the condition. The symptom areas listed above represent developmental systems that have their own neuropsychological features, their own brain–behavior links, and their own gene–environment interaction. Considering the symptom domains individually helps us to understand both etiology and treatment from a multidomain perspective.

Sources of Variability in ASD Symptom Presentation Across Children

The saying, "If you have met one person with ASD, you have met one person with ASD," reflects how different one child can look from another. Yet, for professionals involved in diagnosis and treatment, it is important to examine systematically the dimensions that contribute to variability. Important sources are presented as follows.

Cognitive Level

If there is one feature that perhaps makes the biggest difference in how one individual with ASD appears and functions from another, it is intelligence level. In fact, those with ASD can range from being highly intelligent to having a significant intellectual disability. For those with high intelligence, there is a discrepancy between their intellectual abilities and their ability to navigate the social landscape, but these persons may complete college and beyond. Another variation is "peak skills" and talents that do not reflect an overall high intelligence. Most persons with ASD, whether high or low, or average or somewhat above or below average in intelligence, also have a scattered neuropsychological profile with a distinctive pattern of strengths and weaknesses across verbal, nonverbal, memory, visual, auditory, and various other information-processing subscales.

Cognitive disability may also be related to conditions that are genetic and neurologic in nature but that also give rise to autism symptoms. The prime example is Fragile X syndrome, a clearly diagnosable genetic disorder that creates both intellectual disability and behavioral manifestations. About 30 percent of children with Fragile X can also be diagnosed with autism. There is an extensive list of other neurobehavioral conditions that increase the risk of ASD in addition to intellectual disability.

In a very young child, intelligence level can be notoriously difficult to assess. This area of inquiry belongs to specialists with a broad variety of assessment strategies at their disposal, as well as the experience and clinical judgment to decide when to withhold conclusions until more treatment is given, more language is developed, or more engagement can be gained from the child.

Severity of Autism Symptoms

At the same time, there is a continuum of severity regarding how many and how intense autism symptoms *per se* are for any individual. For each symptom domain listed above, there are a large number of specific behaviors that represent the autism itself. As long as a child has *enough* of them across the symptom areas, then she may meet diagnostic criteria. However, one child can have many more than another. One child may demonstrate autism symptoms in almost everything she does, while another child may also have more typical developmental skills in parallel to her autism symptoms.

Therefore, the combination of how severe or mild the ASD symptoms are with a continuum of intellectual ability will make distinctive differences between children, especially at the more extreme ends of these two dimensions. Figure 2.1 is a schematic showing these relationships, and the diagnostic outcomes often associated with specific combinations of degree of autism symptoms and level of intellectual disability or ability.

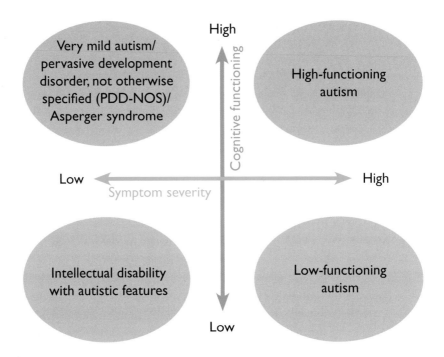

Figure 2.1 The Interface of Symptom Severity with Cognitive Delay

Variability Within the Symptom Domains

Another major source of what makes one child look so different from another child with ASD is variability *within* and *across* these symptom areas of social skills, language/communication skills, repetitive behaviors/ unusual play interests, and sensory behaviors. For the Communication area, for example, there is wide variation in how much language delay the child experiences, and in eventual verbal ability later in life. There may be a number of "atypical" or "autistic" language symptoms for one child—echolalia, scripting—but virtually none for another. One child who does have echolalia may use it for almost everything he says, and another may use it more selectively. This difference in type and severity of given symptoms within a symptom domain contributes to the variability in overall presentation of individual children who are all nonetheless "on the spectrum."

Commonly Occurring Issues that Are Nonessential to the Diagnosis

The abundance of research and clinical focus on ASD has increased awareness of a number of behaviors that are more common for children on the spectrum and that present everyday challenges for them and their parents. For example, many children with ASD have highly restricted diets, such that feeding and nutrition become an important management concern for them. A second common issue is that of difficulty with establishing sleep–wake cycles. A child who is up many times a night with her own ideas of how to pass the time can create a real adjustment problem for the family.

The issue here is that these concerns do not apply to all children with ASD. However, their increased association with ASD may lead to the impression that they are part of the diagnosis. While they are significant management issues, it is important for professionals to know that it is very possible to meet a young child who loves to eat a wide variety of food and who is a great sleeper, and that absence of challenges in these areas does not preclude the presence of an ASD. Just as importantly, feeding and sleeping are significant management issues for children with developmental disabilities in general, not only ASD.

Sensory hyper- and hyposensitivities can give rise to behaviors that are also strongly associated with ASD. These are the broad group of restricted interests and repetitive behaviors that are discussed in Chapter 6. Increasingly, the presence of some type of repetitive or sensory behavior is considered integral to the ASD diagnosis, but this is also an area of great variability in presentation across individuals. Therefore, if a child shows few frank behaviors in this realm, it is important that the clinician not subsequently discount ASD as a possibility. Moreover, sensory behaviors are not the exclusive domain of ASD. They can occur with other significant, non-ASD developmental disabilities. Mild sensory behaviors are very common in children with different learning disabilities and psychiatric disorders as well.

Core Symptoms

Social Interaction, Communication, and Repetitive Behaviors

If young children with ASD can be so different from each other, then what is it that ties them together? For this we refer again to the key symptom domains, and the types of behaviors that are essential to the diagnosis—often referred to as core symptoms.

- In the area of Social Interaction, a child needs to be "missing" the key behaviors that allow him to become engaged with others, initiate social interactions, and carry on sustained social interaction with the child playing an active role in keeping the interaction going.

- In the symptom domain of Communication, the key issue is the use of social language: the ability to use coordinated verbal and nonverbal communication skills to send a message to another person, to "repair" that message if the intended recipient did not appear to receive it, the development of a repertoire of different messages used to regulate the behaviors of others, and the ability to carry on a sustained, reciprocal conversation.

- In the Repetitive Behaviors domain, the child will have delayed and/or unusual play skills as well as some degree of unusual tendency to do things either repeatedly, in strict routines, or based on a relatively narrow set of interests.

Core Symptoms in the Context of Early Development

Three things complicate learning to observe behaviors in very young children that may be related to ASD. The first stems from the fact that the well-known diagnostic criteria for pervasive developmental disorders and autism spectrum disorders in the Diagnostic and Statistical Manual of Mental Disorders, Third Edition (DSM-III) were originally written for children who were somewhat older, because in the past it was very unusual to diagnose this condition under the age of three or four years. Therefore, it becomes necessary to understand and operationalize the earlier *versions* of the behaviors that are (or, as we will soon see, are *not*) present in the preschool- and school-aged child. One important example is core symptom of the inability (or the use of alternate means, eventually) to carry on a sustained reciprocal conversation. However, it is not necessary to wait until a child is verbal to evaluate the specific precursors to this end behavior: Is the child able to vocalize in a back-and-forth manner? Does she use nonverbal and prelinguistic ways to get and keep a communicative exchange going? Does she monitor and respond to the pace and tone of the partner's input? And does she adjust her response based on the content of the partner's message? In fact, developmental precursors of social-linguistic skills are present quite early in the first year of life, really building at 6 to 8 months, refining from 9 to 12 months, and blossoming forth in a more conventionally recognizable way from 12 months on.

The second issue is that children with milder presentations of ASD will acquire some key social-linguistic behaviors before the age of three, but they will be very late compared to typically developing behavior. A good example is that of pointing. Pointing has always been considered an important skill in the social communication area because it functions to direct the attention of another person, and thus it brings in the "social" part of communication. Intentional pointing with the index finger usually appears between 10 and 13 months. Children with milder ASD will eventually discover that pointing may result in an adult giving them something that they want, and/or aggressive early intervention can teach such a skill quite effectively. Therefore, the child may start to point at 20, 24, or 30 months, yet this still represents a "symptom" because of the *late emergence* of a pivotal social-communicative skill. Also, as such skills emerge in the mildly affected child with ASD, they will not be part of a richly developed, integrated repertoire of social, communicative, and play skills (as seems to miraculously occur with little effort in the typically developing child), but instead will usually function to help the child achieve his particular interest goals, which will be generally non-social in nature.

In fact, apart from a specifically regressive period, all children with ASD continue to develop and add skills. Development may be delayed and different, but not stopped. Early intervention can have an extremely important impact by speeding up the rate at which the development proceeds; it also endeavors to alter disadvantageous learning patterns so that more and more effective learning is taking place. The point is that the specific delays and inconsistencies can be a moving target especially because they are occurring during a naturally rapid developmental period.

The third issue relates to the fact that there are distinctively different timing patterns of symptom emergence among children with ASD. At least three patterns have become evident to clinicians and researchers over the years, and new study findings suggest that there are more versions than that. Three general patterns are as follows:

- "Different from the start": Some children with ASD show differences even in the first year in that they may be unusually quiet, not very interactive in terms of exchanging smiles, looks, and vocalizations, and may show a tendency to focus in on repetitive visual stimuli rather than develop a typical early play and object use repertoire.

- "Plateau after the first birthday": Other children will show typical or close-to-typical early social and preverbal development, and often acquire an early vocabulary of up to a dozen words. Then the words drop out and the progress slows to a halt over a few months, and within few a months a more clear autism pattern is in place.

- A more dramatic regression: Other children (usually estimated up to 25–30%) will show typical or close-to-typical early development in the key areas, but then some time in the second year—often between 15 and 18 months—words, eye contact, and social engagement become noticeably diminished over a period of a few weeks. The regression usually proceeds over a few months, and then skills start to build again, but in a clear autism pattern.

Many have wondered "Did the child actually appear 'normal' in early development?" or "Did the caregivers miss seeing symptoms that would have been more evident to a developmental professional?" The use of home movies that became very popular for research in the 1990s has helped to answer those questions. The answer appears to be "yes" to both situations. Reviewing home movies has shown that first-year development can be remarkably free of autism-related behaviors, and parents' reports are quite accurate in this regard. In other instances, early but mild communication delays can be seen, or "whispers" of tendencies show themselves, but not to the extent that a professional would have felt secure in identifying the behaviors as reliably linked to ASD. In this instance, caregivers with little to no background or experience with early development will not have perceived the behaviors as delays or differences. Others will have inklings or impressions but, understandably, do not perceive their significance. Finally, other children did show more specific signs and yet it was not possible for the parents to understand what they might mean. Bear in mind that these issues exist for all types of developmental disabilities that have their manifestations in early childhood.

A final important caveat to round out our understanding of the different developmental trajectories of early symptom emergence is the reminder that ASD can occur side-by-side with other genetic and neurodevelopmental disabilities. Because they contribute their own effects on early development, the patterns become even more varied when other significant disabilities are added to the picture.

The Issue of "Missing" versus More Obvious Autism Symptoms

Only a certain percentage of what contributes to a clinical impression of ASD consists of unusual or frank autistic symptoms. The other percentage consists of what the child has *not* developed in terms of typical early social, language, and play development. Because of the great variability that has been discussed so far, many children will not have a great deal of the prototypical ASD behaviors such as hand-flapping, echolalia, visual stimulation-seeking, and so forth. That is why it is so important to learn the typical developmental foundations of social, communication, and play behaviors in the second and third year of life, because what is "missing" provides the biggest clues to detecting all severity levels of ASD before age three. In the next chapter we begin to survey the symptom domain areas from the perspective of both typical and atypical development and how it relates to ASD.

CHAPTER 3

Communication in Young Children with Autism Spectrum Disorder

In this chapter the key issues in understanding communication challenges and strengths in young children with ASD will be reviewed. First, it is important to understand that children (and adults) with ASD can be quite variable in terms of the *degree* and *nature* of language difficulties they have. However, they will all have one core challenge—using language in a specifically social way. Thus, it is critical to have thorough familiarity with early typical development in this area of social language. Remember, only some of ASD symptoms are frankly autistic behaviors. The rest are the "missing" features of what should be normally seen at a certain age—but the child is not doing them. The observer has to be able to imagine what a child with typical development would be doing in the context being observed.

The communication area is also where specifically autistic or "atypical" behaviors have special significance. Each of these features will be covered.

The "Spectrum" of Language Delay and Difference in ASD

The Continuum of Language Delay in ASD

There is a wide range in degree of language delay and disorder in ASD. The ability to produce spoken words in individuals on the spectrum ranges from being articulate and linguistically talented, on one end of the continuum, to being nonverbal and having great difficulty expressing oneself in a conventional manner (see Figure 3.1). Of course, as in every ability continuum, there are fewer individuals at the extremes and most are somewhere in the middle.

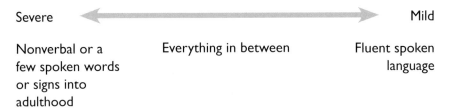

Figure 3.1 The Continuum of Spoken Language Delay in ASD

In young children with ASD, those with the greater degree of eventual language delay will show very significant developmental lags during these early years. Slow progression in acquiring language is probably the most common reason caregivers become concerned about their child's development both when an ASD is present and when there are other reasons for the language delay (Coonrod and Stone, 2004; Hebbeler *et al.*, 2007). (Other reasons are most often either a relatively circumscribed language delay, early manifestations of learning disabilities, or a global developmental delay.) On the most severe end of the continuum, some children will be nonverbal, or acquire a few words and signs over time, and remain that way into adulthood. This certainly does not mean that they will not be communicators, however. The well-developed strategies in the field of augmentative communication and assistive technology (sign language, picture books and communication boards, picture exchange systems, computer-based systems, including voice generation and tablet-based applications) can be applied as early as two years of age. No one needs to be without "a voice."

What does this mean in the context of early development? Obviously, a child who will remain nonverbal will not be speaking during the early and preschool years. Significant delays when a child will eventually be verbal, however, can mean that spoken language starts more toward age four or five. Intensive speech therapy and behavioral approaches can speed up the rate at which a slow language learner advances his vocabulary and communication strategies (Fitzer & Sturmey, 2009).

On the milder end of this continuum, spoken language can range from relatively non-affected to a mild delay such that the child starts to speak between ages 24 and 36 months. Early language, in terms of saying words and grammatically correct sentences, is relatively nonaffected in the specific case of Asperger syndrome. Although there is disagreement in the field about whether or not Asperger syndrome is actually a different condition from high-functioning autism, those who have defined it specify that early language emerges according to the usual timeline (Klin & Volkmar, 2003). As will be described in the rest of this chapter, there will be highly important differences in how that language is *used*; nevertheless, this situation contributes to one end of the continuum of language delay. In other cases of ASD, many children can simply have less intrinsic problem with learning vocabulary, grammar, and syntax.

The Spectrum of Language Delay in ASD

Language and communication challenges in ASD branch out of a simple continuum and into their own spectrum, however, because of the different dimensions inherent in producing language. One such dimension, for example, is the child's ability to physically produce speech. It is possible to understand words and be able to formulate thoughts in terms of language, but not be able to speak one's thoughts easily. Some children seem to have a particular problem using their speaking apparatus (tongue, lips, facial muscles, positioning their palates, etc.) to produce the typical developmental progression of sounds (e.g. babbling and baby talk) and then single words and word combinations. This is called "apraxia" and different speech therapy approaches have been developed to physically help the child form sounds and words. Another example of the independent nature of having language ability but not speaking ability is in nonverbal individuals who can express themselves well with typing. There are a number of older children (and adults) who are nonverbal, but when given spelling board and computers can show adequate vocabularies and conventional grammatical structure. Finally, there are dramatic instances of adults and adolescents with autism who learned later in life to type—adults whose general behavior would not lead the outside observer to think they had the ability to express complex thoughts—and their typed communiqués have shown both impressive intelligence and verbal ability. These significant discontinuities across and within skill areas are one of the reasons ASD is such a fascinating condition.

Some children with ASD have language delays and disorders that look a lot like children with language-based learning disabilities but who do not have ASD. In other words, they may have late-blooming language, struggle with grammar and syntax, but eventually become competent speakers. But soon other language-based tasks trip them up—learning to read, trying to learn a foreign language, and, most typically, having difficulty with higher-level expositional writing. Written language organization, creating cohesive narratives, and expressing abstract thoughts will be particular difficulties.

And just like children without ASD, those with it can have challenges in the area of fluency (e.g. stuttering), voice quality, articulation, and prosody. Prosody, however—how one uses tone of voice, pitch variation, and phrasing to add meaning to their communications—is one area that signals an ASD language difficulty; more about that later (see page 56).

The Subdomains of Language Development

Once again the question becomes: If children with ASD can all be so different in their language learning, what makes them all the same? There is in fact a straightforward answer to this question: the social use of language, or pragmatics.

Language and communication comprises a complex field and requires extensive study to acquire expertise. Speech-language pathologists and academic linguists help us to understand that there are at least three areas that need to develop in an integrated manner for normal language development (see Table 3.1).

The first area, *Form*, refers to the child's ability to acquire a conventional vocabulary, parts of speech, and an intrinsic understanding and use of grammar and syntax. It is the world of verb conjugation, irregular plurals, articles, prepositions, pronouns, subject-verb agreement, conjunctions, compound and complex sentences, clauses, and so forth. The young child's development along these lines is relatively well known and can be mapped out in terms of ages at which different structures are acquired.

The second area is *Content*, which refers to what is being talked about in the child's communication, such as who, what, when, and where, possession, location, existence, re-occurrence, and so forth. Meaning and semantics are notions that relate to the Content area of language. When a child says a phrase about a person doing something, she is talking about an "agent" and an "action." If she talks about Mommy's shoe, she is talking about "possession." As word relationships become more developed and complex, the child also shows her knowledge of "attributes," such as a stove being hot or a chair being heavy. This area covers the rapidly developing internal framework of word classification as well, such as knowing that bees, butterflies, and wasps are all insects;

that airplanes and helicopters and birds are all things that fly. Like Form, this may either be relatively unaffected in the child with ASD, or difficulty with it can impact on the richness and effectiveness of language development.

Pragmatics, or the social use of language, however, occupies a different arena in the child's communicative competence. In order to get others to help you or do what you want them to do, pay attention to you, teach you things, and give you protection, reassurance, affection, and companionship, you must employ an array of communication strategies that go beyond words. In fact, children develop and coordinate these strategies well before they develop many words. What are they?

Table 3.1 The Subdomains of Language

Form	Content	Pragmatics
Grammar	Semantics	Social
Syntax	Meaning	Intentional
Vocabulary	Topics	Regulating
There is a surprising amount of independence among these subdomains in language disorders. In ASD, any given individual can have different abilities in the Form and Content area, but everyone on the spectrum will have significant difficulty with Pragmatics.		

Pragmatics, or the Social Use of Language: The Core Communication Symptom in ASD

The major functions of social language are to (1) regulate the behaviors of others, (2) develop relationships with the help of language and communication, among other means, and (3) carry on sustained, reciprocal conversations. We will focus on the following different clusters of communication behaviors to observe the effectiveness of a child's pragmatics: using and coordinating different modalities of communication, having a variety of types of messages that regulate others' behaviors and keep them involved in interactions, being able to repair a failed communication, and having strategies for keeping a conversation going. In order to accomplish these complex tasks, the child needs to draw upon a variety of communication abilities, understand the give-and-take of the communicative process, and receive and perceive the communication coming from others.

Next we will review four main clusters of communication skills that are key to pragmatic competence.

Coordinating Verbal and Nonverbal Communication Modalities

The true content of our communicated messages often relies less on word meaning than on what is sent through nonverbal means. What are these various modalities at work in the complex and subtle sending of information from one person to another? For our purpose of building observation skills, consider these three modalities:

1. *Verbal/vocal*—what words or sounds are made. Certainly words are an important part of communication, but well before using words, infants and toddlers are able to impart meaning through their prelinguistic vocalizations. In the "preintentional" phase—before the age of about eight months, a parent has learned to interpret vocal tone in terms of the child's state, that is, content, happy, irritated, in pain, frightened, and so forth. From then on a child begins to approximate more specific communications through vocal tone and phrasing, for example, using a tone that is insistent, questioning, angry, or conversational. When words are eventually combined with tone and phrasing, then this feature continues to add essential meaning to communication attempts.

2. *Nonverbal/facial*—eye contact, gaze shifting, and facial expression. Eye contact not only tells the partner to whom the message is being sent, but shifting gaze from an object to a person implies who and what are involved in the information exchange. Facial expression adds an emotive component that casts a highly specific value to the nature of the communication.

3. *Nonverbal/gestures and body language*. Gestures are a highly effective way to clarify and add information to ensure that the message gets across quickly and efficiently. Pointing tells exactly where one should look for more information. Patting, pantomiming, shrugging, swiping, holding out an open hand, and opening and closing a hand are also well used and understood gestures. Postures and stances are excellent ways to send the emotional tone or degree of interest and engagement and thus clarify the nature of the message.

Developing skills in each of these modality areas alone are seen in children below one year of age. Right around one year, the ability to use the different strategies—both sequentially and at the same time—emerges.

In typical development, the ability to smoothly coordinate all three modalities starts around 12 months and is in place by about 18 months. It is often a revelation that such a fundamental and complex system develops so early! But this knowledge also helps us to realize why it is possible to determine a diagnosis of ASD by the age of 24 months.

The pictures in Figure 3.2 show how very young children are able to combine the three communication modalities to be effective communicators. The examples start with a 13-month-old, then a 14-month-old, and continue to children who are two-and-a-half years old.

Girl pointing at crayons
13 months (typically developing)

Gesture + vocal

Boy asking to be picked up
14 months (typically developing)

Eye contact + gesture

Figure 3.2 Coordinating Communication Modalities

Boy asking for his ball

14 months (typically developing)

Child's yellow ball has bounced out of reach
Eye contact + gesture + verbal

Girl showing picture on toy bathtub

20 months (typically developing)

Eye contact + gesture + verbal

Boy asking for bubbles to be opened

24 months (typically developing)

Eye contact + gesture with object
+ verbal

Figure 3.2 Coordinating Communication Modalities *cont.*

Boy asking adult to put toy on the table

24 months (typically developing)

Gesture (patting) + verbal

Boy asking for airplane on shelf

30 months (typically developing)

Gesture + verbal

Figure 3.2 Coordinating Communication Modalities *cont.*

Learning to Observe

It is important to spend time watching young children in order to see how much they use nonverbal and verbal strategies both separately and together. Then, when observing a child suspected to have ASD, the relative absence of this skill will signal the difficulty he or she is having in this area.

In observing a child where ASD is a question, this area—using and coordinating the different communication modalities—is a relatively easy and extremely important area to take note of. However, it is also necessary to be aware of the range of absence vs. presence of these abilities in young children with ASD. Again, we must refer to a continuum of severity that matches up with the general severity level of ASD symptoms in a given child.

- *More severe:* The child rarely shows the ability to combine verbal/ vocal and nonverbal communication. But he may sometimes, and those "sometimes" are predictable: when engaged in his favorite activities, when highly motivated to get something, and more reliably with familiar caregivers and within highly familiar routines.

- *More mild:* The child shows more skill with this area as she develops (usually in the third year of life), especially with intensive treatment, and even more so in the same circumstances as above: with highly favored activities, high motivation, and familiar caregivers and routines.

- Even when mild delays are present in this area, the ability of the child with ASD will never approach a level that looks like a non-ASD child at this young age. There will be very obvious differences in the amount and quality of ability to coordinate different communication modalities.

- There are children who do show mild enough delays in this area so that it is difficult to determine their diagnosis. Of course, that child will have to be examined across all symptom domains, and he may show just enough ability in all areas to make the diagnosis issue very confusing. In these cases diagnosis is usually deferred and treatment recommendations will align with the specific area of need regardless of the diagnostic status.

Specific Issues of Eye Gaze and Gaze Shifting

Using eye gaze for specific functions is so integral to human communication that it is worth spending time discussing a few more details that figure in the development of this general ability.

ALTERNATING GAZE BETWEEN A PERSON AND OBJECT AS AN EARLY FORM OF SPECIFIC COMMUNICATIONS

Around nine to ten months of age, a baby is slowly becoming more "intentional" in her actions. Intentionality means that although the baby doesn't have actual conscious thoughts about it, she has learned that specific actions will have specific results, so that behaviors and timing of them become less random and more directed. The child has learned through experience what actions will get the results she is looking for. One specific communicative behavior is an early version of asking for something by shifting eye gaze between a person and a desired object. As this represents the statement "give me that!" and this kind of statement is called an imperative or demand, the linguistic term is *protoimperative*. The "proto" part refers to an early but not completely formed version of something. Alternating gaze between an object and a person can also function as a comment or statement, such as "I see that." As such a statement is, in grammatical jargon, a declarative statement, this baby version is called a *protodeclarative*.

At the 12- to 13-month point, most children are starting to use vocalizations and gestures to send a variety of messages, so that there is less need to rely on alternating gaze for those messages, so this isolated action begins to drop out.

ALTERNATING GAZE BETWEEN AN OBJECT AND PERSON AND BACK AGAIN

This behavior is used by young children both as a monitoring behavior (to see how the adult is reacting, or if he is paying attention) and to indicate that the partner is supposed to do something with the object (see Figure 3.3). Once established during the early part of the second year, it persists. It is a key indicator that the young child understands that the person and the object are connected in the context of the interaction being carried out. Therefore, this will be seen in children developing typically and much, much less in the child with ASD.

Figure 3.3 Children Alternating Gaze Between an Object and Their Play Partner to Monitor the Other Person's Involvement and Response

See Table 3.3 for a summary of how eye gaze is used in early communication, with approximate timelines.

FOLLOWING THE EYE GAZE OF ANOTHER, FOLLOWING THE POINT OF ANOTHER, AND EXPECTING THE COMMUNICATION PARTNER TO BE ABLE TO DO THE SAME

This is another skill that develops before 12 months of age. Babies appear to have an inborn understanding that there is an invisible trajectory starting at their communication partner's eye and leading to an endpoint that they should look at. In addition to gaze following, the same applies to following a point (see Figure 3.4).

This boy is following the gaze of the adult to look at the same thing she is

These boys are following the point of an adult

These boys are pointing to show

Figure 3.4 Children Following the Gaze and Point of an Adult and Expecting Reciprocation

This seemingly innate tendency to look where their partner is looking or pointing, and doing the same back for them, is one of the key behaviors included in clinical evaluation instruments and in research on joint attention (see Chapter 5) in young children with ASD. It is reliably missing in them until they may develop it through targeted intervention or, in the case of milder children, as they get older and have opportunities to practice it. The fact that it did not come in naturally points to the early gaps in the development of social cognition, which is discussed in the next chapter.

Communicative Intent: Having a Variety of Types of Messages to Effectively Regulate and Engage Other People

This is the second major cluster of communication behaviors that help us to understand how a young child is doing in terms of pragmatics or the social use of language. As a toddler begins to send more messages, the meaning and intent of the messages also develop into a more differentiated repertoire. The child can accomplish an ever-expanding variety of missions with her language efforts. Language experts have generated lists of these specific functions or intentions that include the following:

- seek attention

- request an object

- request an action

- request information

- comment on an object

- comment on an action

- answer

- acknowledge another's communication

- greet

- negate

- protest.

This list begins to make it clear how these statements help the child to regulate the behaviors of others around him, and get his needs met.

Bear in mind that the "needs" of the developing child go past immediate physical needs and comfort. Several of these functions are primarily to engage others in conventional ways (greet, answer a question), and in ways that keep the other person engaged in the interest focus of the child (seek attention, comment, seek information), *or* that keeps the child himself engaged in the adult's focus (acknowledge other's speech, answer). These last two functions are essential for the child to learn language and conventional play.

Importantly, all of these communicative intents can be accomplished prelinguistically—that is, without words—and therefore a speech delay does not account for delays in pragmatic skills. Children with delayed language but without ASD are usually able to use gestures, eye contact, and vocalizations to compensate and thus be effective in getting their message across. The pictorial examples in Figure 3.5 show how to recognize these communicative intents as they occur during an interaction or observation.

Learning to Observe

When observing the communication intent repertoire of a young child at risk for or with ASD, it is useful to have a list of the intentions with you, so that the different intentions can be checked off as they are observed.

Request object

13 months (typically developing)   14 months (typically developing)

Girl requesting crayons   Boy requesting ball

Figure 3.5 Examples of Communicative Intentions

Contrast with child with ASD—Does not request object
30 months (ASD)

Girl and mother are enjoying the "Sesame Street" theme song together. Girl bangs on the piano; mother sings and makes Big Bird dance

Girl reaches out and grabs Big Bird without requesting, making eye contact, or any other communication

Girl continues to make Big Bird dance while mother sings. No eye contact has occurred at any point

Request action
14 months (typically developing)

Boy requesting to be picked up

Figure 3.5 Examples of Communicative Intentions *cont.*

30 months (typically developing)

Boy requesting that a bottle be
opened up

24 months (typically developing)

Boy requesting help from mother

Contrast with child with ASD—Does not request action

20 months (ASD)

Boy wants to leave the park, so he
looks at the gate and whines

Figure 3.5 Examples of Communicative Intentions *cont.*

Request information
20 months (typically developing)

Girl spies a crayon

She picks it up and asks her mother what it is

She looks at her mother while she waits for an answer

Comment on object
20 months (typically developing)

Girl naming brush, baby

Figure 3.5 Examples of Communicative Intentions *cont.*

24 months (typically developing)

Boy noticing cameraman

Comment on action

30 months (typically developing)

Boy commenting about person
coming out of plane

Greet

14 months (typically developing)

Boy waving and saying bye

Figure 3.5 Examples of Communicative Intentions *cont.*

Acknowledge another's speech
30 months (typically developing)

Protest—Vigorous objecting
24 months (typically developing)

Mom: "We can't look at this now. We'll look at it when we come back."
She puts it back on the shelf

Boy pushes his mother's arms away and shakes his arms and body back
and forth, saying, "Aaaaaahhhhhh!" Then he attempts to grab the toy again

Figure 3.5 Examples of Communicative Intentions *cont.*

Contrast with child with ASD—Does not protest

30 months (ASD)

Girl has taken Big Bird from mother during a singing activity and has been making Big Bird dance on the keyboard

In anticipation of the second verse, mother starts to take Big Bird back so girl can play while mother sings

Mother has to pry Big Bird out of girl's hand. Girl does not look at her mother or make any protest or other type of communication

Figure 3.5 Examples of Communicative Intentions *cont.*

Negate

30 months (typically developing)

Boys replying in the negative

Contrast with child with ASD—Does not negate, but responds behaviorally

30 months (ASD)

Girl bangs on the piano while Mom makes Big Bird dance and sing

When the first verse finishes, Mom cues girl to start a second one. Girl does not immediately comply

Then, instead of saying "no" or "not now," she kicks the piano away with her feet. She does not look at Mom or vocalize or verbalize

Then she turns away and involves herself in a different activity. No communication, verbal/vocal or nonverbal, has been directed toward her mother

Figure 3.5 Examples of Communicative Intentions *cont.*

In parallel to coordinating modalities, the development of a repertoire of communicative intents begins around 12 to 13 months, and most intentions are in place by 18 months, becoming more extensive and regular in use by 24 months.

Many children with ASD who are more able with language do acquire the ability to make requests, especially if this has been taught to them. As with all the behaviors that have been and will be presented, these normal developmental benchmarks are rarely completely missing. What distinguishes ASD is that the variety and rate of intentions is significantly lower. A typically developing child may emit intentional communication at a constant rate, if there is an available and engaged partner, and will use a number of different types of intentions over a period of several minutes.

To evaluate the intentional repertoire of a child, it is necessary to note their occurrence throughout the time of observation. It is useful to use a checklist, as well as to create a variety of situations where the child would be expected to show her ability to use one or another.

Communicative Repair: Fixing a Message that Didn't Get Across

In the busy flow of human interaction, a message not reaching its intended recipient happens fairly regularly. The child who implicitly understands that his partner will somehow signal to him that the message has been received will be monitoring that person for a reaction or acknowledgment. If there is no indication that a response is forthcoming, the child with social language skills will employ a predictable set of strategies to repair the failed communication. These strategies are listed below on a developmental hierarchy, such that the earliest ones are listed first and the more mature ones are further down the list.

1. Repeat what is said (or vocalized).

2. Repeat and get louder or use an insistent tone of voice.

3. Add a modality—for example, a gesture.

4. Make a "syntactic" repair—say it somewhat differently.

5. Metalinguistic repair—talk about the fact that the message was not heard.

Observation of a communicative repair can be left to chance during an observation, or it can be probed for in specific ways. The major way is to set up a requesting situation, and then don't respond to the child's request. Figure 3.6 shows processes of communicative repair for a typically developing child.

Girl says, "Water bottle there" (and points to the bottle on floor)

Adult doesn't understand. She thought girl said "sit there." She says, "You want me to sit on the floor?" Girl repeats "water bottle" while looking at the adult, adding eye contact to her repetition

Girl repeats "water bottle" for the third time, but this time she adds a gesture (pointing) to augment her message

Figure 3.6 Communicative Repair

Girl says "Sit there" to her play partner while pointing to a chair

When she doesn't get an immediate response, she repeats her request, getting louder, gesturing closer to the chair, and adding eye contact

Girl monitors the situation to see that she has achieved her goal

Figure 3.6 Communicative Repair *cont.*

In young children with ASD, several different responses can occur when they are challenged with a failed message. If the child has made a request, such as for an object she wants, and the adult does not respond, the reaction of the child indicates her skill and expectation that this situation can be remedied. Therefore, the following reactions can be observed in ASD, approximately in order of lesser to greater skill:

1. The child immediately gives up, indicating that he does not yet understand what to do, or even that direct communication can serve his needs.

2. She physically grabs, pushes, or pulls directly for the object while not looking at or communicating directly to the partner.

3. He repeats his reach or vocalization several times, not adding eye gaze or more specific gestures, before giving up. This persistence signals that the basic notion of communication is being developed.

4. She tries one modality several times, until finally adding another, such as looking up at the partner. Her modalities are attempted sequentially, not coordinated simultaneously, yet this also indicates some foundational ability.

5. Through intervention, the child has learned to use request behaviors and now reproduces it but in a learned way. For example, he sits back and says "Give, please," without pairing it with eye contact. Or he may reach, then when that doesn't work, point as he has been taught, but without eye contact. This learned ability while young is a good start, and can develop in some children into more natural, coordinated communication skills.

Learning to Observe

In order to observe if or how a child repairs a failed message, it may be necessary to set up the situation, such as purposefully not reacting when a request is made, or by violating an expectation within a familiar routine. An example of the latter is to have the parent read a favorite book, but then have her stop and not turn the page when the child would expect her to. As the child indicates that he wants the page turned, have the parent continue to "act dumb" and not turn the page to see what strategies the child uses to repair the communication.

Discourse: How to Carry on a Conversation

The earliest precursor of "talking" back and forth actually occurs at age three to four months. This is the time when the infant loves to watch a caregiver as he smiles and "baby talks" to her, and, when given a chance, will gurgle and make noises back to the adult. This can maintain itself for several turns in most dyads. As the weeks and months go on, the infant gets busy with motor milestones and object manipulation, and this pure conversation recedes, but different exchanges continue in the way of baby song and imitation games, tickling, and peek-a-boo. The ability to take alternating conversational turns appears for the most part innate, although the baby must have a cooperating partner for the behaviors to emerge. These prototypical forms, practiced well before more intentional communication emerges, show that an early foundation for the interactive part of conversation is being formed.

Therefore, knowing how and when to take a turn is the first component of being able to sustain a conversation. The next component is being able to maintain a topic so that the conversation goes somewhere while maintaining some kind of cohesion. Maintaining and extending a topic can happen as long as the child has conversational turn-taking in his repertoire and has enough words and gestures to convey meaning (see Figure 3.7). A 24-month-old is often capable of carrying on a several-turn conversation.

Another essential feature of discourse competence is being able to stay on topic as well as "extend" the topic of conversation. Staying on topic shows the partner that the topic choice is being respected, and extending the topic by taking it somewhere slightly different allows the conversation to keep moving forward. If a person starts a conversation with, "It's raining," his conversational partner may reply, "Yes, it is." But if she stops there, the topic has been maintained but the conversation comes to a halt. If the partner then adds, "And, as usual, I forgot my umbrella," then the conversational initiator can keep going by replying, "Oh, that's too bad," or "I always do that too," or "Well, the forecast didn't call for rain, did it?" or "Do you want to borrow mine?" or any of a multitude of choices of where to take this conversation.

Persons with ASD are known for a number of different tendencies that prevent socially typical conversations from taking place. The first is not to reply at all, either not sensing the need to or else not knowing how to carry on a casual conversation. A second is to change the topic abruptly to one that is foremost in his or her mind, or a favorite topic. A third is to start and continue a one-sided conversation about a favorite topic.

Turn 1

Adult: "Do you have a chicken?"

Girl hands over the chicken, saying, "Chicken"

Turn 2

Adult: "This chicken says woof, woof"

Girl: "The chicken says... The chicken says..."

Turn 3

Adult helps her out: "What does the chicken say?"

Girl: "Bock, bock"

Figure 3.7 Early Discourse: Turn-taking in Conversation, Staying on Topic, Using Eye Contact

Into the third year, discourse skills develop so that the child becomes aware of the "needs of the listener"—in other words, is the conversational partner paying attention, understanding, or giving cues that the conversation is over? These pragmatic discourse skills are those with which older children and adults with ASD continue to have significant challenges. Many social skills intervention programs are aimed at developing and honing these skills.

The young child with ASD will have very few of these abilities that allow him to carry on a spontaneous, extended conversation. Some, however, will be able to engage in familiar and practiced routines of conversation, give answers and choices, and even really enjoy memorized song, word, or gestures games.

Atypical Language

The communication subdomain is one where there are specific, well-known autistic behaviors that may be observed—those that are referred to as "atypical." Atypical behaviors are those that cannot be explained by delays, but instead by unusual differences. They are behaviors that are never "normal," regardless of when they occur developmentally.

Importantly, these frank communication autism symptoms are not present in every young child on the spectrum. When they are, however, they are also very important red flags for the presence of ASD. They are described as follows:

Echolalia

Echolalia is the term used to describe when the child repeats what the other person says. However, there are many different forms and degrees of severity of echolalia. In terms of types, echolalia is usually divided into "immediate" and "delayed." When the child repeats what the communication partner says right after it is said (immediate), she may be doing so either as an automatic, noncommunicative response, *or* as a way of answering or responding.

Like many other symptoms in ASD, echolalia can be present in a milder or more severe way. The most severe would be that the child uses echolalia for most of what he says, and it may or may not have communicative function, that is, to impart some information to others. Less severe is when echolalia is used in addition to some words, signs, and gestures. The mildest is that echolalia is used occasionally to respond to the partner's communication, and the child has functional language to some degree.

A certain amount of echolalia occurs during typical language development. The child may repeat the last word her caregiver says, as a kind of placeholder while she formulates what to say, or as a short answer or response. The difference with the typically developing child is that she also has a wide variety of expected skills developing at the same time, and this transient echolalia is just one of many strategies the child has in her repertoire.

Finally, echolalia can play a role in a child with a non-ASD language delay, and may persist longer than the phase of the child with no language challenges at all. Again, in this instance it will not occur along with all the other signs and symptoms of ASD communication, especially the selective delay in pragmatics.

Scripting

In scripting the child repeats pieces of dialogue he has heard on a video or TV. It seems to be a more elaborate form of echolalia. Its degree of severity mirrors that described for echolalia—the child can use scripting for the majority of what he says, and it can be all done "to himself," or, on the other hand, as an unusual but somewhat effective way to communicate. It can be done during times that are appropriate. An example is a child who drops something and then exclaims, "Oh bother!" as modeled after Winnie the Pooh. Or, as his mother asks him to come downstairs, he says, "I'm coming, I'm coming!" with all the same inflection as in the Cinderella video. Echolalia of favorite characters often accompanies a restricted interest in the show or its characters (see Chapter 5).

Instrumental Communication

The child may act physically on the adult to get what she wants, without the more social communication cues that typically accompany requests, especially eye contact. The child may push and pull the adult, either taking his hand or pushing him from behind. Another form of instrumental communication is to pick up the adult's hand and place it where the child wants something done, invariably done without eye contact or vocalization; this is referred to as *hand-leading* (see Figure 3.8).

Instrumental communication

Girl takes her mother's hand and places it on the mouse instead of asking her mother more directly to continue the computer game

Figure 3.8 Instrumental Communication: Hand-leading

Not surprisingly, some instrumental communication occurs in typical development, often around the stage where the child has some words but often not enough to say everything she wants to, when she wants to. The difference from ASD will be that the phase is transient and there are many other typical communication skills in place as well.

Highly Indirect Communication

Here the child goes through physical routines that he has learned may result in his goal. An example is standing by the refrigerator when he wants something to eat, but not calling attention to himself. When the adult sees the child standing there, she opens the refrigerator and offers him something to eat, or he gets it himself. Another example is a child who, when she wants to go out, puts her shoes by the door, then stands there with no other attempt to get someone to help her. The parent soon discovers her, and says "Oh, do you want to go out?" The child smiles and sits down to have her shoes put on.

Unusual Babbling or Jargoning

The child may use sounds and strings of sounds that are outside the usual repertoire of phonemic, or speech sound, development. Repetitive babbling that is not the more typical jargoning, causes some parents to remark that their child has a "language of his own." Other types of unusual sounds are high-pitched vocalizations, grunting, and squealing.

Differences in Prosody

Here the child uses atypical patterns of tone and pitch when speaking. When younger, this may be sing-song, breathy, or a rising pitch at the end of every phrase. A slightly older child may use a monotone, and sound robotic, and this is the most common type of prosody difference in older children and adults.

Summary

Individuals with ASD have language delays that range from severe to very mild, but all have significant difficulties with the social use of language, or pragmatics. Pragmatics is the feature of communication that regulates the behavior of others and engages others interpersonally. There are several important sets of pragmatics competence behaviors to observe (summarized in Table 3.2). The first is the child's ability to coordinate verbal and nonverbal communication modalities to optimize his message. The second involves the development of a varied repertoire of communicative intentions. These two pivotal areas of social communication ability have precursors in the first year of life, but blossom around 12 to 13 months and grow to completion by 18 to 24 months. Children with ASD will have very significant lags in these abilities, although they do better in the context of familiar routines with familiar caregivers. A third way to gauge pragmatic competence is to observe the ability of the child to repair a failed communication. The final way to understand how a child is doing with social language is to observe whether she is able to carry on a sustained conversation, which entails, at minimum, being able to maintain and extend a topic. The communication symptom domain is one in which this is a set of atypical behaviors to look for. These atypical language features include echolalia, scripting, instrumental communication, highly indirect communication, atypical babbling or jargoning, and unusual prosody.

Table 3.2 The Elements of Pragmatic Communication Competence

Coordinating Communication Modalities	Using a Variety of Communicative Intentions	Communicative Repair	Discourse (Conversation) Skills
Verbal/vocal: • Words or meaningful sounds • Variable and interpretable intonation Eye contact and facial: • Eye contact used in several specific ways during communication • Varied facial expressions give specific meaning to message Gesture: • Increasingly conventional gestures enhance meaning of message • Body language does the same	Child uses a variety of intentions frequently throughout the day: • Seeks attention • Requests object or action • Comments on object or action • Protests • Negates • Requests information • Greets	If child does not get a satisfactory response, he tries again in a variety of ways: • Repeats message • Gets louder • Changes intonation • Adds gesture, vocalization, or more eye contact • Syntactic repair: change words or word order • Metalinguistic: uses words to comment about not being responded to (older)	Child sustains conversation of a few turns using specific skills: • Knows when to take conversational turns • Maintains topic • Extends topic • Understands the partner's role in the conversation
Timeline			
8–12 months: Each modality is developing and two can be coordinated 12–13 months: Child begins to coordinate all three 15–18 months: Child coordinates all three smoothly and frequently	8–12 months: Protoimperative and protodeclaratives, Requesting, Protesting 12–18 months: Child uses most intentions 24 months: All intentions used	Emerges same time as requests and other intentional communications	Prototype at 3–4 months, conversational turn-taking from 12 months on

Table 3.3 Ways Young Children Use Eye Contact in Communication

8+ months (to adulthood!)	Looking at the person while vocalizing or gesturing to indicate that the person is the intended recipient of communication
9–12 months	Looking back and forth between an object and person to request the object or have the other person regard the object
12+ months	Looking at a person while vocalizing and gesturing (coordinating communication modalities) to enhance the effectiveness of communication attempt Looking back and forth between an object and person to monitor that the person is looking at the correct object Looking back and forth between an object and person while vocalizing or gesturing to specify that the person is expected to do something with the object

CHAPTER 4

Social Interaction in Young Children with Autism Spectrum Disorder

Difference and delay in social development is at the absolute core of ASD. In the last chapter, we saw how communication delay in terms of learning language itself can be more or less affected in individuals with autism. But this is not the case for social abilities; they are always affected and never "almost normal." Likewise, in the communication domain, the social use of language is always affected, even when vocabulary and grammar may be more intact. There is, of course, a continuum of severity in terms of how completely missing various social skills are, with some children less severely affected than others.

To understand what constitutes social ability and disability, however, requires detailed study. Everyone has his idea of what is meant when a child is said to be very "social" and "related." Yet to come to a conclusion about what symptoms the child is showing in this area, it is necessary to parse out the general construct, breaking it down into more specific, observable behaviors. The material in this chapter uses clinical research findings that have shown which behaviors are the most important to focus on in ASD.

The Social Life of the Typically Developing Child

A child's social life begins soon after birth, when innate infantile behaviors have the capacity to elicit caregiving behaviors on the part of parents or those who feel caring toward the baby. A distressed sound coming from the child may result in her being held, rocked, or fed, and the baby's calmed or satisfied reaction sets off a continuing cycle of signals and responses that, in most circumstances, creates the parent–child bond necessary to sustain the extended caregiving that primates and humans require.

Within a month or two, as a baby's eyesight extends past his nose and as control over eye, head, and neck muscles develops, the child develops a strong preference to look at faces as opposed to inanimate objects (Mondloch *et al.*, 1999; Turati, Simion, Milani, & Umilta, 2002). By six weeks, in addition to intense looking, most children begin to smile and coo in response to adult faces and social input. By three to four months, a baby can carry on an extended exchange of smiles with eye contact and varied vocalizations with a caregiver (Tronick, 2007).

Through these means the baby is able to extract a strong commitment from a few devoted caregivers. It is certainly in her best interests to do so, as her very survival depends on these persons supplying intensive resources in the form of food and physical care and protection. As well, in order to learn the basics of communication and interpersonal behavior, the infant must rely on a constant coach, interpreter, and teacher.

Because of its primal necessity, therefore, social competence is being developed from the earliest days and growing in complexity and intentionality over the first two years of life. These highly developed behaviors can be observed in children whose social development is following a typical course and can be noted to be off-course in young children on the autism spectrum.

However, it is important to recall the various patterns of symptom emergence that different children on the spectrum display (see Chapter 2). Some children show normal first-year social development and then start to lose those skills in the second year, while other children evidence delays right from the start.

The behaviors to be described and illustrated in this chapter fall into the following three general clusters:

- *Social engagement and interest*: How does the child show that he is interested in others and ready to be engaged? To this end, where does the child place himself physically so that he has the opportunity to get involved with others? How does the child use eye contact to signal interest in engagement, and monitor the faces of others to extract information about how the interaction may go? How does the child get social interaction going with others, and how does he respond when others initiate social interaction with him?

- *Emotional signaling*: How does a child exchange purely emotional information with others, and signal her internal state?

- *Capacity for interaction*: How easily does the child fall into a give-and-take pattern across a variety of circumstances, from predictable and scripted routines to a free-flowing, reciprocal social interchange? Can he sustain an interaction once it is started?

Social Engagement and Interest: Specific Behaviors that Imply a Child's Social Motivation and Basic Capacities to Engage with Others

Physical Proximity: How "In the Mix" Is the Child?

In order to interact, a child needs to be close enough to observe what others are doing, get their attention, insert herself into the action, and monitor the reactions of others. Children with ASD are known to go off on their own and pursue their own interests (see Figure 4.1). It is important, therefore to observe whether a child spends more time alone than with others who are accessible to her over a period of time.

What the child is doing while off by himself is an important component as well. Young children with ASD may have unusual sensory interests or repetitive behaviors that preoccupy them. Children without ASD who are very interested in how things work may also choose solitary pursuit of their play, but over the course of time will check in with others and engage in brief age-appropriate social interaction. In contrast, the child with ASD will either avoid or be indifferent to attempts to interact with him.

As with all other ASD symptoms, isolated physical proximity associated with lack of social interest runs along a continuum of severity. At the most severe end is the child who actively avoids being close to where others are, and responds to approach by others by moving away. Others, however, are able to *tolerate* proximity and parallel activity. Still others can engage in some back-and-forth or interactive routines as long as they are those with which they are practiced or familiar. Departure from the familiar routine, or insertion of novel material, may result in the child retreating, however.

Typically developing

Puts self in position to interact with and observe others

ASD

Physically separates self from others

Figure 4.1 Social Engagement Behaviors: Seeking or Avoiding Proximity

Eye Contact: Looking at Others and Monitoring the Eyes and Faces of Others

Eye contact, or rather the lack of it, is one of the most well-known symptoms of autism. However, simple presence or absence of eye contact is not the most useful way to think about this behavior in relation to ASD. It is more useful to consider how the child is *using* eye contact. Some children with ASD do in fact look at others' faces with regularity, yet still do not use that eye contact in typical or effective ways. In order to be judged as "effective" or not, eye contact has to be considered within the following specific contexts, not on its own (see Figure 4.2 for some examples).

1. *Very early protoimperative and protodeclarative communication.* This was discussed in the previous chapter (see page 35). Starting around nine months, a child may request that an adult either get for her, or look at in shared interest, an object or event by alternating her eye

gaze between the object and the person. This subsides in typically developing children in the second year of life as they get better at coordinating pointing and vocalizations and eye gaze to make the same type of requests.

2. *Looking at a person* in combination *with other communication modalities to enhance the effectiveness or the meaning of the message.* This is also described in the previous chapter. Looking at the person makes it clear to whom the message is being sent, and alternating the gaze between the person and the object emphasizes what is being requested (see pages 35–36). As well, because emotional content is sent through the eyes and facial expression, directing a gaze may add information about the child's emotions regarding the exchange. For example, the facial expression may be playful, relaxed, urgent, annoyed, or anxious. Having this information available to the recipient of the message will allow the subsequent interaction to go in the right direction, and in the direction that allows the needs of the child to be met (when the caregiver is able to understand and respond to these subtleties of the message).

3. *Monitoring faces and eyes for social information.* This may be one of the most important behaviors to note in a young child at risk for ASD, because it signifies the presence of key social understanding on the part of the child. Figure 4.2 shows why a child might be monitoring someone's face during an interaction, and what type of information he may be looking for. First, there is the emotional or affective information available: Does my play partner's expression show approval? Is this going OK? Should I keep doing this? Did I do the right thing? Second, the play partner's face may be showing cues about what to do next—is he looking expectantly so that I should take my turn next? Is it time for me to imitate him? What is meant to happen next?

As a side note, one line of research has shown that children and adults on the autism spectrum tend to look at non-social information in pictures and movies, and if they look at people's faces, they often look more at the mouth than at the eyes (Falck-Ytter & von Hofsten, 2011). These studies of course suggest that this is happening during daily interactions, and that those with ASD are not "wired" to look for social information. In addition, informal reports from individuals with ASD have made it clear that sometimes to make eye contact is very overstimulating and sometimes distracting and anxiety-provoking. Whether avoidance of eye contact comes from lack of interest or from avoiding aversive overstimulation, this tendency still results in the missing of social information that is sent from eyes and faces of others.

4. *Following the gaze of another person.* Looking where your play or communication partner is looking gives you very concrete information about where to look in order to continue the interaction effectively, and to get the information you need out of it. This behavior is not solely social in nature, and that is why milder or older children with ASD can eventually add this to their repertoire, especially when they come to learn that the partner can help them play with or learn about things that are of interest to them.

5. *Alternating gaze between object and person during an interaction.* This occurs very frequently in interactions with typically developing children, and seems to serve a variety of purposes. It is primarily a type of monitoring so that the child keeps track of what is happening with the object or activity, and of what the partner communicates through her eyes and face about how this activity is going to move forward. Functionally, it serves to let the play partner know that both the partner and object is getting the child's attention. There are times, as well, that the glancing from object to adult and back is part of what the child intends to happen. For example, a child may hand the person a toy, looking back and forth between object and person, as a way of saying, "Take this."

6. *Social referencing.* This term refers to when the child looks to the adults to get affective information about something novel that has been presented. Studies have shown that if a very young child sees something new that he is uncertain about, he will look to the parent to see how she is reacting, and then react in a similar way (Striano & Rochat, 2000). The standard experiment was to present a small robot that made noise, then ask the mother either to look afraid or smile and look happy about seeing the robot. In most circumstances after the baby looked to his mother to find she was afraid, the baby became afraid and sought comfort from the mother and avoidance of the new toy. If the mother looked happy and welcoming, the child relaxed and wanted to play with the robot.

General

Typically developing

Frequent and appropriate eye contact

ASD

Avoids eye contact

Contexts for observing effective use of eye contact: (1) Combining eye contact with other communication modalities to make the message more effective

Typically developing

Boy makes eye contact with his mother as he raises his hands to be picked up

Girl points, looks, and verbalizes at the same time. There is no doubt to whom she is speaking and where she wants her to look

Figure 4.2 Social Engagement Behaviors: Use of Eye Contact

ASD

Boy, wanting to leave the park,
looks at the gate and cries instead
of looking at his mother and saying
"open"

ASD

Girl takes her mother's hand and places it on the mouse without looking at her
instead of verbalizing her request and making eye contact

Figure 4.2 Social Engagement Behaviors: Use of Eye Contact *cont.*

Contexts for observing effective use of eye contact:
(2) Monitors eyes and faces for social information

Typically developing

Watches other's face for social and communication cues

ASD

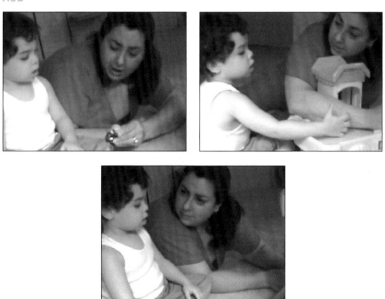

Does not monitor faces and eyes

Figure 4.2 Social Engagement Behaviors: Use of Eye Contact *cont.*

Contexts for observing effective use of eye contact: (3) Follows gaze or point of communication partner

Typically developing

Follows gaze or point

ASD

Does not follow point

Figure 4.2 Social Engagement Behaviors: Use of Eye Contact *cont.*

Contexts for observing effective use of eye contact:
(4) Alternates gaze between object and person

Typically developing

Boy's use of eye contact shows that he intends for the adult to be involved in what he is doing in his play

Typically developing

By looking back and forth between the bowl and the adult, girl shows that she expects the adult to take it from her

Figure 4.2 Social Engagement Behaviors: Use of Eye Contact *cont.*

Learning to Observe

When assessing how a child is doing with eye contact, it is important to observe how the child is using eye contact across a number of contexts. Monitoring faces is as important a social behavior as eye-to-eye gaze, as is gaze shifting in specific situations.

As can be seen, then, understanding whether a child is using eye contact appropriately needs to be appraised from specific interactional contexts. Young children with ASD can show a lot of variation in eye-contact symptoms. Only in some children with ASD is eye contact almost completely missing across contexts; when this is the case, it is a very strong red flag regarding a potential ASD diagnosis. Here are a number of other variations that occur:

1. The child will have reduced eye contact in general, but more will be seen when she is highly motivated to achieve a goal.

2. More eye contact (and positive affect) will be seen during chasing, peek-a-boo, and wrestling games.

3. More eye contact will be seen with familiar caregivers and during familiar routines.

4. Children will begin to use more eye contact with intensive early intervention, although ASD symptoms persist in general; more mildly affected children will show the most rapid improvement.

Making Social Initiations: How Does the Child "Get Things Going" with Another Person?

The most common way that a very young child (12–18 months) engages an adult is by handing him an object (see Figure 4.3). From a developmental viewpoint, this behavior serves multiple purposes. For example, it appears to be an important part of acquiring object knowledge, as a child will hand over the toy and then watch what the adult does with it. Another early behavior is the "show-not-give" of a child under 18 months. This seems to be a way to get the name of the object and/or a bid to interact around the object. One way or the other, these social bids often lead to exchanges of varying lengths.

Social initiation is one of the obviously absent behaviors in children with ASD. The child does not approach others for the purpose of having an interaction, even though the adults or children are clearly available. However, many, including those relatively severely affected, will learn to approach adults for a desired object or action. An important difference is that they will not use eye contact and other communication modalities in the way expected. In addition, once the object is obtained, the exchange will be over. Finally, it would not be unusual for a child with ASD to approach an adult with whom he has established, fun routines, such as rough-housing.

Learning to Observe

When observing a child to understand her social functioning, avoid attempting to directly engage the child at the beginning of the encounter. Most young children need time to become accustomed to the presence of an unfamiliar adult. This also gives the opportunity to see if the child approaches spontaneously and of her own initiative.

Typically developing

Hands adults objects to start an interaction

ASD

Occupies self—does not initiate socially

Figure 4.3 Social Engagement Behaviors: Making Social Bids or Initiations

Responding to Social Initiations of Others

Obviously, the child who is developing interaction skills needs to be able to respond to the social bids of others in addition to initiating them. There are a number of ways to respond, including looking, vocalizing, moving closer, or emitting some action that is a specific response. This is also a set of behaviors that is notoriously missing in the child with ASD (see Figure 4.4). A well-known red-flag behavior is not responding to name, yet this is just one of many ways that the child with autism does not react to attempts to engage him.

Typically developing

Gives an appropriate response to adult bid

ASD

Occupies self—does not respond to social bids socially

Figure 4.4 Social Engagement Behaviors: Responding to Social Bids of Others

Emotional Signaling: Sharing Emotion and Signaling Internal Affective States

Sharing Affect or Sharing Emotions

This behavior is often mentioned as one of the negative symptoms or "missing" behaviors associated with the social features characterizing ASD in young children. Affect sharing occurs when the child is happy or excited and turns to the play partner to share that feeling through a positive facial expression (see Figure 4.5). This can entail the child simply sharing a smile, or, in effect, a "moment"; it can also be accompanied by clapping and laughing such as after an accomplishment (e.g. building a tower or blocks).

Similar to other social features being discussed in this chapter, only the most involved or affected children with ASD *never* share affect. The circumstances where it is seen are the same as those described for eye contact above: sharing affect will be seen around highly favored activities and routines, with familiar caregivers, and in children with milder ASD. Although the behavior will be seen in some circumstances, it will not occur at the rate that it does for non-ASD children, nor will it occur reliably across settings.

Typically developing

Children sharing a moment with their adult play partner

Typically developing

Boy turns to his mother to share a laugh

Figure 4.5 Emotional Signaling Behaviors: Sharing Emotions

ASD

Most children with ASD respond with happy emotion and often better eye contact to tickling, rough-housing, and chasing games

Figure 4.5 Emotional Signaling Behaviors: Sharing Emotions *cont.*

Learning to Observe

To understand a child's range of social functioning, be certain to include observations of the child with a familiar caregiver as well as interacting with the child yourself. Children always show their best levels of sharing affect, eye contact, and direct communication with familiar caregivers with whom they have familiar routines.

Signaling Affect or Emotions on an Ongoing Basis

While turning to another person and sharing affect is an active way to express emotion, children also constantly signal their internal state on their faces without much conscious effort, and without specifically directing it toward another person. Child development research has shown that using the many facial muscles (50+), the basic emotions of anger, disgust, fear, happiness, sadness, and surprise are registered and interpretable on the face of children in the first few months of life (Camras & Fatani, 2008). As the child develops, she is able to signal (and experience, presumably) double and blended emotions, as well as eventually to gain control over which emotions she signals (e.g. trying not to cry, smiling insincerely because it may be expected).

In contrast, a hallmark of the child with ASD is "flat affect." This means that the child maintains a neutral expression without clearly readable emotions most of the time (see Figure 4.6). As with the other symptoms being mentioned, there is variability in what degree this is seen in an individual child. Most children with autism will show strong upset when they are fearful, very frustrated, or hurt; in the same way, they will show happiness and delight given their very favorite activities. What remains a departure from normal is the extent to which they show many emotions in between. If a typically developing child is observed over time, he will signal a wide variety of basic to complex emotions, including wariness, shyness, anticipation, concern, frustration, delight, and calm focused interest. These "shades of gray" are usually what is missing in the child with ASD.

However, one characteristic feature of children with autism is that they do easily show delight when they are involved with rough-house play, bouncing, tickling, and chasing and peek-a-boo games (see Figure 4.5). It is remarkable to see a child of nearly three years of age who does not signal much emotion until this type of activity is begun. Along with expressions of affect, this is also when much better eye contact and turn-taking can be seen.

Typically developing

Boy showing displeasure at having toy taken away

Boy showing delight

Boy showing shyness or self-consciousness

Figure 4.6 Emotional Signaling Behaviors: Signaling Varying Affect

ASD

24-month-old at his own birthday party

28-month-old opening Hanukkah presents

30-month-old on Christmas morning

Figure 4.6 Emotional Signaling Behaviors: Signaling Varying Affect *cont.*

One further caveat involves a subgroup of children with ASD that actually have somewhat outgoing, sunny personalities (see Figure 4.7). They have no hesitance to look and smile at others, are often happy to be around people, and love the baby-level interactive games. They may even approach and greet adults and older children. The important difference in their social functioning is that their interactive skills stop at the greeting level, and at allowing themselves to become involved in physical games. As we have seen, social interaction involves a well-developed set of skills that are intentional and coordinated; these particular children do not have the skills in place to sustain social interaction at their age level.

Figure 4.7 There Is a Subgroup of Children with ASD Who Have Sunny, Outgoing Dispositions

Capacity for Interaction: Imitating and Turn-taking

The capacity for these two key behaviors is seen very early in life. At ages three to four months, babies can take turns vocalizing and smiling at their parents, and are helped to do this when the parent pauses and waits for the child to respond, listens to her, then takes his turn again when the baby pauses. As the months go on, parents from all cultures engage the child in turn-taking games that may involve vocalization or gestures (peek-a-boo, patty-cake). The child's inborn ability to imitate also creates opportunities for the caregiver to perform some action, wait expectantly or encourage the child to do the same thing, and then wait while the baby takes her turn, after which both share delight—which appears to be a reinforcer to the child.

Babies will also imitate gestures in a back-and-forth pattern quite early. In the first weeks, some reflexive imitation takes place. A six- or seven-month-old will imitate a gesture already within his repertoire such as patting the hand or banging a spoon on a surface. Soon other objects become involved in the back-and-forth routine, such as rolling a ball. A child between 12 and 14 months can usually roll a ball back and forth a couple of turns. The object and routine used will depend on what the parent has chosen to coach, but by the second year, the turn-taking capacity has been developed via early imitative games such that the child quickly recognizes the turn-taking context and expectation (see Figure 4.8).

A seven-month-old hands an object back and forth with the adult

Figure 4.8 Social Interaction: Back-and-forth Routine

Learning to Observe

To observe how a child understands turn-taking, it is useful to start
with basic routines and then move to novel activities. Does the child
understand how to toss or roll a ball back and forth, or roll a car
back and forth? If she can do these well-practiced routines, then try
a novel approach such as rolling a plastic ring back and forth and
see if she can adapt to that. Keep adding novelty as well as language
to observe where the understanding of turn-taking drops off. Also
try using prompts ("Now *you* do!") as well as leaving prompts out.

Imitation and ASD

Consider how central imitation is the developmental and learning process of any age child, from infancy on. How would a child learn the majority of conventional play and language if he could not imitate (see Figure 4.9)? Yet, in ASD, one of the central components for imitating is missing to some degree—paying attention to others, watching what they are doing, and the motivation to be like them. Imitation *per se* is considered something that is often missing in children with ASD, but in fact there is a lot of variability (Rogers, Hepburn, Stackhouse, & Wehner, 2003). The variability that occurs, however, is that some children with ASD can imitate others if they are interested in the objects and activities. But the imitation will be limited to objects, and not social behaviors. Nonetheless, children with ASD with some imitation in place are in a good starting place to add more and more behaviors through direct teaching, prompting, and modeling. Those that do not have imitation in place have to first be taught to imitate.

16-month-old imitating adult

Figure 4.9 Social Interaction: Imitation

Turn-taking

As described, turn-taking back and forth undoubtedly gets nurtured in the first year through both directly imitative as well as interactive routines (such as patty-cake, or "How big are you?" or "Where's your nose?"). As the child matures cognitively between 12 and 24 months, she becomes more flexible in taking turns spontaneously with new material rather than the specific routines in which she is practiced (see Figure 4.10). Caregivers continue to teach turn-taking with natural verbal prompts such as "Now *you* do," or "Your turn!" and then waiting expectantly.

14-month-old taking turns with adult

Figure 4.10 Social Interaction: Turn-taking

Summary

Social functioning is always significantly affected in ASD. Core symptoms include difficulties with social engagement, affective signaling, imitating, and turn-taking (see Table 4.1 for a summary). Social engagement is compromised when a child does not place himself within the social action and does not look at others' faces or monitor faces for information about how to proceed with interaction. Eye contact serves specific functions across a number of communication and social contexts (see Table 4.2 for a summary). Furthermore, children with ASD do not easily initiate social interaction or respond to social bids by others. Differences in affective signaling include affect sharing—sharing smiles and excited happiness during times of heightened arousal—and the capacity to signal facially a broad variety of emotions. Children with ASD are less able to convey their internal state through facial expression and thus appear "hard to read." Finally, children with ASD are usually less prone to imitate others, a skill that plays a central role in learning language and play. A related skill selectively affected in ASD is that of taking turns. Although turn-taking appears to develop naturally in typically developing children, those with ASD do not understand the pacing and timing of it to the same extent.

Table 4.1 Components of Social Behaviors in Young Children

Degree of Social Interest		Emotion Signaling		Turn-taking	
Typical	*ASD*	*Typical*	*ASD*	*Typical*	*ASD*
Stays physically close so that interaction and monitoring of behaviors can occur	Goes off by self or tolerates proximal activity without monitoring others	Shares emotion when excited or happy	Emotion-sharing may be absent or restricted to highly favored activities	Imitates across many types of behavior Can take turns in a variety of circumstances	Reduced imitation or restricted to non-social actions May be absent or limited to routines and favorite activities
Gives eye contact and monitors faces during interaction	Reduced eye contact and especially reduced monitoring of faces	Has a variety of facial expressions that signal emotional state in an ongoing way	Has reduced variety of facial expressions; is "hard to read"	Acts reciprocally: adjusts response according to what partner just did	Great difficulty making spontaneous adjustments

Table 4.2 Ways Young Children Use Eye Contact Socially

Social monitoring	Watching the face of another to look for cues for turn-taking and about approval or affective state of partner
Social referencing	Looking at the facial expression of adult when something novel is presented in order to understand how to react
Gaze-following	Following the gaze or point of another due to an implicit understanding that there will be something of interest there
Gaze-directing	Directing own gaze or point to object or event of interest with implicit assumption that the other person will also direct attention toward it
Gaze alternation	Alternating gaze between an object and another person signifying the expectation that the person will be attentive to the object and/or what the child is doing with it

CHAPTER 5

Putting It All Together
Sustained Social Interaction, Joint
Attention, and Reciprocity

In the last chapter we saw how social competence can be broken down into discrete behaviors that accomplish engagement with others on physical, practical, and emotional levels. Of the several social areas that are affected in ASD, one or the other may be less so in an individual child; or, as was discussed for each component, children with ASD show better skills in highly familiar and specially favored activities, and with familiar caregivers. Yet, ultimate appraisal of whether the social and social-communication levels are sufficiently impacted to lead to an ASD diagnosis hinges not on an individual behavior, but how they are orchestrated. True social competence remains a very challenging goal because it calls for using *all* the different social and communication skills in a coordinated, ongoing, interactive, and flexible way. A young child with ASD will not be able to accomplish this, regardless of how mildly affected he is, or how relatively intact an individual social skill component is.

Sustained Social Interaction Calls upon Multiple Social and Communication Skills

Consider the interaction between a 26-month-old girl and an adult illustrated in Figure 5.1.

Girl initiates gesture/song routine

Adult joins in

They continue together

Adult introduces next part of song

Girl follows her lead

They continue together

Adult speaks next part of song as child observes

Girl takes her turn

Figure 5.1 Sustained Social Interaction: Girl and Adult

In this simple and rather short exchange, the girl accomplished the following social components described in Chapter 4: social initiation, social response, eye contact, sharing positive affect, displaying readable positive affect facially, imitation, and turn-taking. It helps to have a well-practiced gesture-rhyme routine to facilitate the interaction, and some young children with ASD can accomplish some features of the routine—but not all the social parts of it as well as everything coordinated smoothly. In addition, this girl can accomplish non-routine social interactions with the same ease.

When the interaction is not based on a game-like interaction with a prescribed back-and-forth script, then communication becomes integrated into the exchange as well. The exchange shown in Figure 5.2 occurred between a 30-month-old boy and his mother.

Recalling the list of communicative intentions in Chapter 3, this little boy used the following during the exchange: comment on object, comment on action, acknowledging other's speech, and answers. His social interaction skills included: social initiation and responding, sharing affect and eye contact, happy, readable expression, and turn-taking. Again, this was all accomplished in a rather rapidly paced, smoothly coordinated way.

Learning to Observe

To determine if a child at risk for ASD can accomplish sustained interaction, start with very familiar, scripted routines as advised by the parents. As the interchange is repeated, change small things to see if the child will insist on only doing the prescribed parts. With familiar and favorite routines, a child on the spectrum may also accomplish more shared affect and eye contact than at other times. Challenging the child with new variations will then impact the degree to which social features are being demonstrated by the child.

The boy (30 months) is experiencing a viewfinder for the first time

He spontaneously shares it with his mother

He even turns the viewfinder around so it is properly oriented for the other person

He takes his turn again

He spontaneously shares again

Figure 5.2 Sustained Social Interaction: Putting It All Together

He takes his turn again

He takes his turn again

He spontaneously shares again

He continues on for six more turns!

Figure 5.2 Sustained Social Interaction: Putting It All Together *cont.*

Joint Attention: Two (or More) Individuals Paying Attention to the Same Thing for a Period of Time

Joint attention is a key construct in understanding ASD and how it affects learning. Very similar to the construct of sustained social interaction presented here, it is not a single behavior but a set of behaviors that function to keep the child and another person focused on the same activity. Perhaps the conceptual significance of joint attention is what it accomplishes as an end state, and therefore its importance for social, language, and conceptual learning. For it is within the context of joint attention that a majority of language and conventional play is learned. Many research studies have demonstrated that the ability to engage in joint attention is a predictor for how well a child with ASD will do as time goes on.

There are both narrow and broad definitions of joint attention. The narrow definition, which is used in research studies and clinical observation assessment systems, is where the adult draws attention to an object with eye gaze or pointing gestures, and if the child follows the gaze or the point, she is scored positive for joint attention. Another somewhat broader definition is that two individuals are paying attention to the same thing or mutually involved in the same activity. The broadest definitions include both having a joint focus but also maintaining it by using eye gaze, shared affect, communication behaviors, gestures, and all the other things considered so far in this book.

The main reason joint attention is considered such a pivotal skill in ASD is that its absence is both a diagnostic feature (he has autism, in part based on the observation that joint attention is missing) *and* an explanatory feature for why typical learning is not taking place (he is not learning language and conventional play because he does not have joint attention).

To explore these concepts further, first consider some skill areas less dependent on social interaction. When it comes to gross motor behavior, for example, a child mainly needs the *opportunity* to be safely physically active in a number of situations. She requires open spaces to crawl, some objects to safely pull up onto and cruise along (the coffee table usually suffices), uneven surfaces to negotiate, steps to climb, different movement experiences to develop balance and the sense of her body moving through space, and gradients of challenges in these areas that match the next level she is ready for (often found at the playground). The parent can enhance the experience by modeling specific movements, creating interactive physical games, and providing enhanced means of practice (such as walking on a balance beam), but in the absence of these directed experiences, the typically developing child will nonetheless develop adequately, given the inborn drive to move and explore in the context of an adequate and benign physical environment.

The same is true of fine motor skills: when the child is given various objects to manipulate on a continually challenging gradient, basic competence does not depend on one-to-one interaction. As with gross motor development, competence can be enhanced by increased and specialized opportunity, but it is not necessary if the child is intact neurologically and the environmental opportunities are adequate. Both these developmental domain areas also are affected by genetically endowed greater or lesser ability along a "talent" continuum, and both can be affected through experiences that directly impact on the child physically, such as accidents and disease.

Given the comparatively non-social requirements of these areas of development, it is not surprising that a number of children with ASD are relatively unaffected in motor skills, or may even be especially able, for example, in terms of fine motor dexterity.

In contrast, a child cannot develop communication without an active communication partner, one that is present from even the earliest weeks and months. (Well, as can be seen with many children with ASD, they can learn how to speak, count, and spell from *Sesame Street* and videos, but not in a socially appropriate way.) Interaction with an adequate partner develops both the process and content of language and communication. In the context of joint attention, a child learns words for objects, actions, events, and attributes; when that context includes play, this learning is multisensory—as the child touches, hears, and sees the objects and action—and active—as the child acts on the objects. Input from the communication and play partner affirms the child's actions and observations, and, of central importance, introduces and elaborates new ideas that build language and play concepts. The pictures in Figure 5.3 show how typically developing children incorporate material provided by the adult.

Boy is putting a toy car with a toy driver down the ramp

As the car comes out the chute, the driver falls out of the car. Boy says nothing

He picks up another car with two drivers, starts to put it down the ramp, and says, "Here come the boys…"

Adult supplies elaborating material: "I hope they don't fall out"

As the toy car comes out the chute, the two toy drivers fall out

Boy's comment shows that he has incorporated an idea from the adult

Figure 5.3 Joint Attention—Child Incorporates Material from Adult: Boy and Adult

Children with ASD Can Achieve Non-social Joint Attention

Importantly, based on the somewhat narrow definition that two people are paying attention to the same thing, many young children with ASD can achieve this state if there are not additional social/communication demands occurring. This may be seen when a bright, very motivated child with ASD is fascinated by specific learning areas, and he comes to understand that an adult (or sometimes older sibling, cousin, or neighbor) can help support him in his play and learning. This will invariably be in visually based tasks such as puzzles and visual-spatial activities. As well, when a child with ASD has a strong special skill, such as learning numbers, letters, and spatial patterns, his motivation to do this activity overcomes any aversion to doing it with another person, as long as the person does not stress the child with social demands. The fact that it is possible to pay attention to the same thing and interact around it without calling upon social and communication skills makes it important that the definitions of joint attention be precise in assessment and intervention applications.

Boy loves to have his dad help him with his alphabet puzzle by handing him each piece in order

Boy enjoys having his Good Night Moon book read by his dad, as long as he reads it the exact same way each time

Figure 5.4 Joint Attention with Low Social Demands

Reciprocity: What the Child Does Depends on What Her Partner Just Did

Both the areas of social communication and social interaction have, as a subcomponent, the ability to take turns. In early development this starts off with imitative and ritualistic games. It was discussed earlier that the turn-taking evolves from routines to the implicit understanding that many situations have a back-and-forth pattern to them. Typically developing children monitor their partners for cues about when they should make their next move and what it should consist of. As time goes on, increased experience and flexibility allow the child to set the agenda and direct the activity as well.

Children with milder ASD will learn, on a delayed timetable, any number of routines, and good memory skills often will allow them to follow the steps precisely. Children with more severe ASD will do so when they get older, such as school age. Herein lies the issue. Children with ASD are known to be especially motivated to follow predictable, familiar sequences and are likely to become upset if a step occurs out of place. But what typifies well-developed social interaction into the second year of life is *reciprocity*, which is characterized by ongoing adjustments based on the content of each person's input.

Reciprocity can only be achieved when the child is engaged in the activity with another person and both share awareness of the broader theme of the interaction, which allows for detail changes that remain consistent to the context. Let's consider again that the adult and child are playing with the farm and plastic animals. It has been agreed that nighttime is coming and it is time for the animals to go back to the barn. The child walks his cow back, but the adult says, "My sheep is so hungry, he is going to eat some more grass first!" The child has the opportunity either to carry on with his original idea, or turn his cow around and say, "Hungry, too!" while having the cow make eating sounds. Or, this violation of the expected course can stimulate communication and idea development when the child says, "No! Go to bed, sheep!" and this nonetheless is a reciprocal response because it is directly related to what the play partner just did and said.

The example shown in Figure 5.5 illustrates lack of reciprocity. The interactions of the child with ASD demonstrate how the child stays on his own agenda, not responding to input from the parent.

Probing for reciprocal interactions uses the general concepts of inserting novel ideas and observing if the child integrates it into her activity, and of violating the expected sequence and observing if the child attempts to repair it.

Mother and boy are exploring a box of toys together

Mother calls his attention to a car but he does not respond

Mother calls his attention to a toy figure…

Boy looks at it…

takes it from his mother…

and drops it into the bin without a comment

Figure 5.5 Child with ASD Showing Lack of Reciprocal Interaction: Boy and Mother

Boy points to an object at the bottom of the bin and says "Square"

Mother picks it up and shows him that it is a play waffle

Boy does not pick up on his mother's idea and repeats that it is a square

Eventually boy decides on his own that it is time to sit inside the toy bin

Mother tries one more time to draw his attention to the play items

Boy takes it from her...

and drops it in the bin without picking up on the play theme

Figure 5.5 Child with ASD Showing Lack of Reciprocal Interaction: Boy and Mother *cont.*

CHAPTER 6

Repetitive Behaviors in Young Children with Autism Spectrum Disorder

This area has come to include a very broad set of behaviors. They range from very physical ones such as whole-body rocking and spinning, to more internal, idea-based behaviors such as topic obsessions. In between are visual self-stimulatory interests, such as watching fans spin, strong interests in mechanical workings, and excessive adherence to routines. This chapter will present a system of organization for these behaviors to help the observer obtain a systematic accounting of those which a child may be demonstrating.

The Nature of Repetitive Behaviors in the Young Child with ASD

What Ties Disparate Behaviors Together

Although the behaviors that fall under this broad category are highly variable, they all have in common that they are repetitive or restricted and/or to some degree "self-stimulatory." They are repetitive in the sense that the child performs them over and over but without the typical variation or elaboration that occurs in developmental play. They are restricted in that they do not occur within a broader, varied repertoire of interests and play skills that develops naturally in most children. For example, some young children with ASD get "obsessed" with a character such as Thomas the Tank Engine, and prefer to play with such toys over any others, and memorize all the names of the characters, when similar skill is not seen for any other topic. This is, then, a restricted interest. Other children show remarkable abilities in naming letters and numbers—far above their age level—but do not show other, simpler play skills typical of their peers, and this is restricted as well. They are self-stimulatory in that they appear to be done for the purpose of seeking comfort, interest, arousal, or sensory homeostasis, and not for social or communicative purposes.

Variability Across Children with ASD

There is tremendous variability in how much of this behavior occurs, and which ones are seen, in young children with ASD. Some research suggests developmental changes from toddler to school age, with different patterns depending on the type of repetitive behavior (Richler, Huerta, Bishop, & Lord, 2010). Then, certain children show their autism features more prominently in the social and communication symptom domains, with virtually no clearly unusual behaviors in the repetitive behaviors domain (Walker *et al.*, 2004). The way that all very young children on the spectrum *will* show disturbances related to this area— in the absence of frank self-stimulatory behaviors or not—is that they will have underdeveloped imaginative play, restricted play themes, and a tendency toward repetitive play (doing their favored activities over and over).

Understanding Play Development in Young Children

In order to understand that a child is not developing typical play patterns, it becomes necessary to learn about object and play development in the first three years, and to do so requires directed effort and study. (This situation parallels the early social-linguistic skills that were covered in previous chapters.) For example, it is common for a clinician to observe a two-year-old child pretending to feed a doll or stuffed animal by putting a spoon to the doll's mouth once or twice, and then note that that the child "has pretend play." Yet, this level—which is a single-step, isolated play action—is only at the 12- to 15-month level. Even a 12-month-old can typically put a phone to his ear and make a noise like he is saying something into the phone. By 18 to 24 months of age, the typically developing child can accomplish multi-step pretend sequences, direct play to self and others, use increasingly nonrealistic props while understanding that they still represent the original object, combine objects and actions in increasingly complex ways, and so forth.

In addition to representational and symbolic play, a young child on a typical course develops an increasingly differentiated play repertoire that includes several categories of play. This may include visual-spatial play (puzzles, blocks, building); books; crayon and paper; manipulatives such as clay and dough; sand and water, ball, and outdoor play; and pure imaginative play. There is plenty of room in normal development for different talents and interests across these categories. Thus, it behooves the observing professional to seek out this knowledge as she proceeds to apply it to observing children at risk for disabilities.

In the same way, familiarity with how a child usually elaborates his play in an ongoing way is necessary in order to make a judgment about whether a child is being "perseverative" rather than "persevering." More descriptions on this topic are presented below.

On the other hand, all types of repetitive behaviors that are seen in older children and adults *do* occur in many children on the spectrum below three years of age. Which particular ones that occur are child-specific, and within individual children they may come and go, or one type of repetitive behavior may have its phase and then be replaced with a different one. The next section describes the range that exists before extensive examples are provided.

Learning to Observe

The observer needs to be familiar with the content and sequence of play in typically developing children from about nine months to three years to understand when play is not emerging in a normal pattern in toddlers. Although many young children on the spectrum may not have frank repetitive behaviors, they will demonstrate repetitive play that is underdeveloped for their age, and that favors visual-spatial interests as opposed to imaginative play. It is important to take a survey from the parent of all the child's play interests, to see how broad versus restricted her interests or skills are.

The Subtypes of Repetitive Behavior in ASD and Versions Seen in Young Children

Researchers have made attempts to create classifications of repetitive behaviors using the standard approaches of clinical observations, statistical techniques, and combinations of these two approaches. One major distinction that has been made is between "higher" and "lower" self-stimulatory behaviors (Turner, 1997, 1999). The lower ones are considered those that involve direct physical and sensory stimulation: rocking and spinning, head-banging, spinning wheels, flicking lights on and off, feeling textures over and over, and smelling things. The higher ones involve strong personal preferences, such as those based on routines and rules, as well as ideas, such as obsessions with certain topics, math, TV characters, and so forth.

Factor-analytic approaches have produced anywhere from one large factor to five to seven factors (Kim & Lord, 2010; Lam, Bodfish, & Piven, 2008; Mooney, Gray, Tonge, Sweeney, & Taffe, 2009). The several-factor solutions do approximate the distinction between sensory-based behaviors and more idea-based behaviors. The subtypes as presented below fit basically a five-factor model, but with behaviors that are particular to very young children. The organizational model is illustrated in Figure 6.1, and individual behaviors are shown through pictures throughout the chapter.

WHOLE-BODY BEHAVIORS	VISUAL BEHAVIORS	REPETITIVE PLAY	SEEKS SAMENESS	HIGH INTEREST AND ABILITY

Spinning, twirling, rocking, jumping, hand-flapping, toe-walking, and pacing	Moving head and body for visual effects, looking out of side vision, looking closely at objects, looking at edges, making things spin, flap, or wave and watching them; finding visual events in the environment: fans, mechanisms, lights flashing, credits rolling	Doing the same simple activity repetitively; manipulating mechanisms, parts of objects, and simple cause-effect events; watching the same video or reading the same book repeatedly; making patterns by lining up and stacking objects	Wanting to follow the same route in the community; insisting on sameness in daily routine, clothes, food; carrying same object around	Special skills in letters, numbers, shapes, recognizing logos; special skills in art and music; character and topic obsessions

More sensory-based

Figure 6.1 Restricted and Repetitive Behaviours in Young Children with Autism Spectrum Disorders: An Organizational Model

Whole-body Behaviors and Motor Stereotypies

Some children like to move their bodies in repetitive ways, and the most typical forms of this include spinning and twirling (spinning self as well as twirling on swings), rocking back and forth while seated or standing, jumping and hand-flapping, pacing back and forth, and banging the head against a chair, the bed, or the floor (see Figure 6.2). Many experts think that these types of behaviors come from sensory disturbances, particularly in the child's system that senses what his body feels like while moving, and he seeks constant motion to even out a hyporeactive response to proprioception and movement (Ben-Sasson *et al.*, 2007). This sensory feature is addressed at more length in the next chapter. Another movement behavior that is strongly associated with ASD is that of walking on tip-toes; it is not clear if this stems from how it feels to hold the body in that position or if hypersensitivity on the bottom of the feet leads to it.

Rocking back and forth

Spinning and twirling

Figure 6.2 Whole-body Behaviors

Jumping and hand-flapping

Running and pacing

Figure 6.2 Whole-body Behaviors *cont.*

One of the more dramatic manifestations of physical repetitive behavior is self-injurious behavior (SIB), or that which can cause self-harm. This includes self-hitting, biting, head-banging, picking at skin, or poking at eyes. Fortunately, frank SIB is rarely seen in very young children, as it tends to develop as a child gets older, but only in a minority of individuals with ASD (Dominick, Davis, Lainhart, Tager-Flusberg, & Folstein, 2007).

Visual-stimulation Behaviors or Stereotypies

A large number of visual repetitive behaviors are seen in individuals with ASD, and these occur in young children as well. To enable the observer to take a systematic inventory, they are broken down as follows. (See Figure 6.3 for examples in each category.)

Visual Effects Produced by the Child's Own Movements

Some children move their head around, appearing to watch what it looks like when they do this. In the same way, they may enjoy the visual patterns that they see when they twirl on a tire swing, or when they spin themselves around, or rock back and forth. A particular behavior that has been noted is the tendency to look at things out of the peripheral vision, and then moving at the same time. Examples are running next to a picket fence or iron railing while looking out of side vision, or running by a reflective surface and watching the effects.

Mirrors seem to hold a fascination for some children on the spectrum, and in particular while they are moving in front of it. They may perform dance, exercise, or gesture-song movements, or just jump up and down, for example on their parents' bed while looking at themselves in the dresser mirror.

Finally, a common visual self-stimulatory behavior is to wave hands or wiggle fingers in front of the eyes.

Visual Effects with Objects: The Child Creates the Effect Herself

Probably the majority of visual repetitive behaviors involve a child manipulating an object in a way that presents an interesting repeated effect from her viewpoint. Starting with looking at things out of the peripheral vs. central vision, some children pick up objects and hold them to the side while looking at them out of their side vision.

Children with these visual interests may spend lots of time making things spin, flap, jiggle, and wave through various inventive ways. The following is a list, which is illustrated in Figure 6.3:

- spinning the wheels of toy cars

- dropping things such as lids or plates on the floor and watching them spin until they come to a rest

- making something round spin on a surface with a flick of the wrist and watching it

- lying down on the floor and rolling a toy vehicle while closely watching the wheels spin

- finding a surface at eye level, like a table or chest, and doing the same (rolling the toy vehicle)

- dangling things from a string

- flapping and twirling a string, pipe cleaner, or piece of cloth in front of the eyes

- holding a flag, cloth, or sock in front of an air conditioner or heater and watching it wave

- watching water run from the faucet or through fingers

- flushing the toilet and watching the water swirl and flow

- sifting sand, wood chips on the playground, rice, or dried beans through the fingers and watching this visual pattern closely

- noticing the edges of things—tables, ledges—and looking closely at them or running the hand along them while moving.

Another version of visual stimulation is a strong preference for cause-effect toys that create light (and often sound) effects when a button or some other mechanism is pushed. The child may do this repeatedly. Another version of this is flicking light switches on and off repeatedly. These behaviors have overlap with the repetitive play category.

Another visual-stimulation behavior with objects involves a child holding something of visual interest very close to his eyes. This may be combined with some visual topical interest, for example, the logo on the side of a crayon. He may pick up each crayon and visually inspect it very close to his eyes, before putting it down and picking up the next crayon.

Visual Effects with Objects: The Child Finds the Effect in the Environment

In other cases, the child is drawn to visual events, already occurring, that she discovers in her home, school, or neighborhood. A common example is a spinning overhead fan. The way the light comes through a window, a reflection, or the way traffic looks passing by the window are things a child will focus on. Other times children are drawn to visual spectacles on television, including letters that light up on game shows, or a spinning wheel with numbers on it. Some children love to watch the credits rolling at the end of a video, and are more interested in this than the video itself.

Effects the child produces with his own body

Shaking head for visual effects

Watching self in mirror while moving

Figure 6.3 Visual-stimulation Behaviors

Visual interest while moving

Waving fingers in front of face

Effects the child creates with objects

Making things spin and watching them

Figure 6.3 Visual-stimulation Behaviors *cont.*

Spinning wheels on toy cars

Making things flap and wave and
watching them

Sifting things (chips, beans) through fingers to watch them fall

Figure 6.3 Visual-stimulation Behaviors *cont.*

Watching water run (by itself or through fingers)

Effects the child finds in the environment

Shapes, letters, numbers, and character animations on computer screen

Numbers, letters, spinning wheels, flashing lights on TV game shows

Credits rolling at the end of videos

Overhead fans

Looking out the window at cars going by

Figure 6.3 Visual-stimulation Behaviors *cont.*

Repetitive Play: Perseverative Activities, Focusing on Mechanisms and Parts of Objects, and Creating Patterns

Repetitive Play as Reflected in Perseverative Activities

One play pattern that may be seen in young children with ASD is the tendency to pursue a relatively conventional activity, but do it over and over again without developing and elaborating the play. An example would be completing a favorite puzzle, then dumping the pieces out and doing the puzzle again several times in a row. Other examples are dumping out crayons and putting them back in the box, or putting pennies in a toy bank and taking them out and repeating the process over and over again. These activities are frequently visual-spatial and may also involve some special interests and talents involving letters or numbers or shapes, or favorite characters or themes.

Books and videos figure into this tendency as well. A child will ask for a favorite book to be read several times in a row, but it must be read in the exact same way each time. Likewise, a favorite video is asked for incessantly, and the child can easily watch the whole thing through repeatedly. Out of doors, a child may find her way to the sandbox and then fill and dump the sand over and over again; throwing stones in water repeatedly may hold attention for a long time (see Figure 6.4).

Another version of repetitive play is to find objects in the home environment and then manipulate them in unconventional and repetitive way. A 13-month-old girl found a big plastic bag full of crumpled plastic bags, and tossed it around for many minutes. One child found a metal tape measure and spent many minutes throughout the day pulling the measure out and watching it snap back. It is possible that the combination of the numbers on the tape measure as well as the cause-effect mechanism made this irresistible to her. Another child would methodically tear pieces of toilet paper off the roll until he was sitting in a big pile of fluff.

Child performs activity over and over again without elaboration; it may be difficult to transition him to a different activity

Boy tearing toilet paper

Girl with measuring tape

Boy throwing stones in the water

Figure 6.4 Repetitive Play Behaviors 1

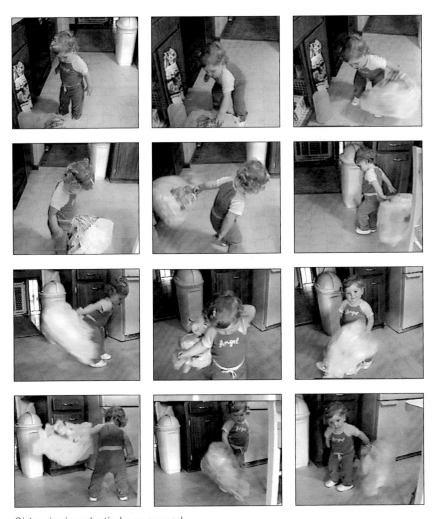

Girl swinging plastic bags around

Figure 6.4 Repetitive Play Behaviors 1 *cont.*

Boy lines up his Winnie the Pooh characters on the bathtub ledge

Then he knocks them back down…   and then lines them back up again; he proceeds to do this several times in a row

Boy wants favorite book read over and over without variation   Boy causes stacking ring to rock back and forth repeatedly

Figure 6.4 Repetitive Play Behaviors 1 *cont.*

Interest in Mechanisms, Parts of Objects, and Cause–effect Events

The larger tendency in this category seems to be that of focusing on mechanisms and direct demonstrations of cause-and-effect. Thus, many children with ASD are drawn to opening and closing doors, manipulating lock mechanisms, and noticing the mechanical movement of things. As well, they are known to be interested in playing with "parts of objects," for example, focusing on opening and closing the door to a toy car or toy barn rather than playing with the toy conventionally. Push buttons and other switch mechanisms on household electronics, appliances, and toys similarly hold an interest and may occupy the child much more than other more conventional play activities (see Figure 6.5).

The computer, tablet, and touch devices seem to hold a particular interest for young children on the spectrum. The immediate cause-and-effect experience, the visual (and/or sound) response, and the affinity for mechanisms as opposed to more unpredictable language and social interaction seem to "stack the deck" for this type of technology offering so much appeal.

Interest in mechanisms and parts of objects that can be manipulated repetitively, and simple cause-and-effect events

Repeatedly manipulating parts of objects

Turning light switches on and off

Opening and closing doors repeatedly (actual doors or parts of toys)

Pushing buttons on toys that create light, sound, music

Manipulating household electronics and appliances

Figure 6.5 Repetitive Play Behaviors 2

Creating Patterns: Lining Things Up and Stacking Objects

This play interest is rather well-known as a red flag for ASD, and is striking when seen (see Figure 6.6). The child methodically makes a visual pattern for herself by lining up things in a row—they may be toy cars and vehicles (all of which must face the same way)—plastic animals, blocks, or her favorite set of characters from a Disney movie. Or, cans are taken from the cupboard and stacked up, as are the child's blocks or nesting cups.

Stacking objects repeatedly

Lining things up

Figure 6.6 Repetitive Play: Creating Patterns

Learning to Observe

Many repetitive behaviors may look like what any other young child might do, such as dropping the lid of a container to watch it spin. To differentiate a repetitive behavior from a typically developing one, the observer needs to ask the following questions: How much does the child repeat this without varying the strategy? How engrossed or mesmerized is he during the activity, and does he protest when he is interrupted? What other activities are in the child's play repertoire, that is, how fully developed is it across play categories?

Seeking Sameness in Routine and the Environment

In this area of repetitive behaviors, the notion of sameness for the sake of sameness is at play rather than a particular sensory experience, motion, or object. Another way of viewing this strong preference is that change itself is not well tolerated. The concern for sameness and predictability can range across situations and routines. One child can have many "sameness rules" across many daily situations, and another may have only selected ones. On the other hand, some children on the spectrum are rather easygoing in their routine and go along with changes without much more problem than the average child. The range of issues can be seen in the following descriptions.

Wanting to Travel the Same Route in the Environment

A child may be very aware of the route taken through the community during her various travels. If a different turn is taken, she may get very upset. Sometimes part of her interest comes from wanting to see a favorite logo (McDonald's) or sign as much as wanting the route traveled to be the same. If a child is really interested in numbers and letters, for example, then she may anticipate her favorite street signs and route signs (e.g. Route 46). As well, certain children on the spectrum have a good ability to understand the spatial features of their larger physical environment, and in fact are interested in preserving sameness in their actual route. These children may eventually become interested in bus and subway routes and in maps.

Keeping Sameness in Daily Routine

Once the child perceives the order of his day, either at home or at a nursery program, he may hold that sequence very dear and insist that he always hangs his backpack on the same hook, always sit in his particular chair, and that his familiar schedule be adhered to. Changes in routine, such as new babysitter or a substitute preschool teacher, are upsetting and disorienting.

Keeping Sameness in Clothes, Food, Colors, and Objects

A child may settle in on particular clothes and refuse to wear different ones. Sometimes this is based on texture (due to sensory sensitivities; see Chapter 7) or preferred character logo (due to strong character interests; see below), or strongly favoring certain color, or simply due to wanting to preserve the sameness and predictability. This may then apply to cups, dishes, or utensils used. In problems with restricted food intake, difficulty with change and novel foods *per se* can play as much a part as texture and taste selectivity (Koegel *et al.*, 2011).

Some children with autism keep sameness in their environment by carrying around a particular object with them. These objects are usually not toys but a somewhat idiosyncratic choice—Dad's discarded wallet, a plastic green triangle, or a silk flower. They may also carry around an object that they like to perform a repetitive behavior with, such as a cloth or string.

Areas of High Interest and Ability

This final area encompasses the special interests for which individuals on the autism spectrum are well known. However, it may be less well known that these types of unusual abilities and focused interests can be present in very young children and are part of the diagnosis, as they are considered restricted and repetitive behaviors (see Figure 6.7).

Early interest and ability in letters and numbers

Precocious ability with puzzles

Early interest and ability in music

Character and topic obsessions

Figure 6.7 Areas of High Interest and Ability

Special Skills and Interest in Letters, Numbers, Shapes, and Logos

It is striking to see an 18-month old who has virtually no language and relatively few age-level play skills, but who can correctly point to each letter of the alphabet when asked. This may also occur with numbers and shapes. Regardless of the age of the child, when these abilities are significantly above other general skills, this constitutes a "peak skill." The child with the early interest in letters may or may not go on to sightread and spell before the age of three, which is referred to as hyperlexia. This reading ability is almost never accompanied by comprehension, however, at least not in the form where the child can elaborate on what she has read or do anything more than perform the reading task.

A given child may also have advanced abilities with numbers, starting by recognizing and naming them, and sometimes continuing on to manipulate them arithmetically. Similarly, the child may start by recognizing numbers on a clock and become interested in telling time. The same holds for shapes—a boy who is behind developmentally in many other ways loves to do shape puzzles and can name advanced shapes such as trapezoid and hexagon. Some children show peak skills in all of these areas and others favor just one or two.

The excellent visual discrimination and strong memory skills involved in these talents sometimes applies to logos as well. A child can go through the grocery store and recognize and call out all the cereal brand logos. Another child will come to recognize all the car logos—Toyota, Hyundai, Jeep, Chevrolet, Ford—and call them out as he sees them coming 100 feet away.

Special Abilities in Art and Music

Some adults with autism are celebrities for having advanced ability in drawing, painting, and music. Although true "savants" are very rare, it is not unusual to see a certain level of talent in children, or certainly striking ability when compared to their other delayed skills. When it comes to music, the child may perk up and engage with music or song when she generally does not respond to language. A child who does not speak very much may be able to recite or sing whole verses of a nursery rhyme song. Skills in drawing, color, and composition can also be seen as a child approaches three and above.

Character and Topic Obsessions

Winnie the Pooh, Thomas the Tank Engine, Blue's Clues, the Wiggles—these characters may become of great, enthusiastic interest to certain children. Again, while they are not picking up other conventional skills in the area of language and cognition, they nonetheless have memorized the names of all the characters of their favorite shows as well as different features about them. Children who "script" (see page 54) may use dialogue exclusively from their favorite shows.

Children who are character-focused may favor the associated books, videos, toys, and action figures, as well as clothes and backpacks bearing the logos and likenesses, so that they refuse to engage with other things not involved with the character. As they begin to speak, they may want to talk more about the character than other topics.

Sometimes children on the spectrum who have this tendency have serial obsessions and will eventually leave one behind and take up another. As a child gets older and learns more things, he may develop the strong interests that older children with ASD are known for: sports statistics, weather phenomena, cars, mechanical things, geography, subway and bus routes and schedules, to name just a few.

Appreciating the strong preferences and talents of young children with ASD can be important in designing teaching programs that motivate an individual child. Some talents, such as in music, art, visual-spatial abilities, mechanical workings, and math, may prove to be life-long strengths.

Summary

Restricted, repetitive, and stereotyped behaviors comprise a very broad set of different behaviors, ranging from more sensory-based to more idea-based. The sensory-based involve moving the body a certain way and seeking visual experiences that are self-stimulating. Repetitive play is a subtype wherein the child takes a relatively conventional activity but performs it again and again without changing or developing it in some way; lining up and stacking toys is a related behavior. Seeking sameness, or resisting novelty or change, is also considered a type of repetitive behavior and manifests in many different forms. Finally, "peak skills" that are above the child's other developmental skill levels may show themselves in abilities with letters, numbers, and shapes, recognizing commercial logos, completing puzzles, music, and art. Character obsessions, such as with cartoon and video characters, also result in knowledge about the character at a level above others being shown by the child.

CHAPTER 7

Sensory Behaviors in Young Children with Autism Spectrum Disorder

In the last chapter, the sensory features of repetitive behaviors were addressed when discussing physical and sensory self-stimulatory, repetitive behaviors. It is sometimes difficult to distinguish between a repetitive behavior and a sensory-based behavior, and there are undoubtedly circumstances where it serves no purpose to make the distinction. However, sensory seeking and avoiding reactions are well known to occur at a high rate in autism spectrum disorder (Boyd *et al.*, 2010), and they present themselves at times quite independently from repetitive behaviors. Their presence is not essential to the diagnosis, and sensory challenges are associated with a number of other non-ASD disabilities. Nonetheless, in ASD, they seem to be especially frequent and especially marked in degree, and they can cause significant disruption to the daily routine for the child and family.

A major feature of sensory-based behaviors and reactions is that they operate as "two sides of a coin": both over-reactions and under-reactions are considered manifestations of sensory disturbances. Under-reactivity is seen as leading to the child seeking out extra, stronger experiences to integrate into his system what he is lacking from routine exposure. On the other hand, over-reactivity is usually interpreted as the cause of avoidance or fear and anger when confronted with the sources of input.

Sensory Behaviors Associated with Movement

Seeking Movement

Some children with ASD engage in extra movement experiences, which can manifest in high activity level, running, and pacing. Clinicians have suggested that a child craves movement when she doesn't "feel" herself or her body as she moves through space as much as other children do. The hallmark repetitive behaviors, such as spinning, rocking, and twirling on swings, may be associated with this need. This child may also love to swing at the park, and parents are impressed with the length of time the child can spend on the swing, and how fast and high she likes to be pushed. Movement-seekers may also go down slides insatiably, as well as being drawn to any situation where they are "going forward fast," such as in amusement park rides. A similar expression of this need may be when children love being tossed in the air, swung, tickled, and chased. Some children "come alive" during these rough-house games whereas they are slow to engage with many other activities (see Figure 7.1).

Spinning

Twirling

Swinging

Running and pacing

Slides

Figure 7.1 Sensory Behaviors: Seeking Motion

Park rides

Bouncing

Being thrown around while rough-housing

Rocking

Figure 7.1 Sensory Behaviors: Seeking Motion *cont.*

Avoiding Movement

Other children have a very difficult time with movement. This is the child who may hold on with white knuckles to the swing ropes, and likes to stay close to the ground. Clinicians may use the term "gravitational insecurity" and support them by giving them small amounts of movement close to the ground and building up to more over time.

Sensory Behaviors Associated with Touch

Seeking Touch

Seeking deep pressure is common to see in a young child with ASD. It is assumed that a child seeks tactile experiences because he does not experience touch against his skin or body in the same way as other children (see Figure 7.2). Whether or not this is the explanation, a child may frequently seek hugs and wrestling from caregivers, push his head and body against furniture, and squeeze himself into small places. Children may also find something that vibrates and hold it against their cheek or body.

Another way that children show extra attention to touch is through a focused interest in exploring textures; for example, rubbing their hands over carpets, sweaters, plastic bristle blocks, or whatever has caught their interest. They also may create their own tactile experiences by taking texture objects and rubbing them on their skin.

Child burrows his head into the corner of the couch

Child likes to crawl on his parent

Child seeks strong hugs from parent

Figure 7.2 Sensory Behaviors: Seeking Touch

Child plows his head into the carpet as he crawls along

Child creates a tactile experience for himself

Figure 7.2 Sensory Behaviors: Seeking Touch *cont.*

Avoiding Touch

Some children are considered "tactile defensive." The very same child who seeks out deep pressure may also have an aversion to light touch, and especially that which is unexpected or not self-initiated. Sometimes aversion to sensation against the skin translates into difficulties with clothing and bed linens. The tactile defensive child with clothing sensitivities typically reacts strongly to clothing tags, seams, and scratchy textures. She may insist on wearing only certain types or items of clothes. These children may also try to keep clothes off them, and are constantly undressing themselves when younger (see Figure 7.3).

One of the most challenging behaviors that can accompany ASD in young children involves feeding problems, many of which stem from difficulty with textures experienced while eating. A child under one year may have difficulty going from pureed food to that with lumps in it. In the second year and beyond, some children restrict their intake to a few key foods, causing concern over nutrition. Not all feeding problems in ASD stem solely from hypersensitivity to textures, but it often plays an important role.

Child does not want sand on his hands

Child bothered by tags

Figure 7.3 Sensory Behaviors: Avoiding Touch

Sensory Behaviors Associated with Smell and Taste

Seeking Smells and Tastes

Some children with ASD are known to frequently smell things, as well as to lick objects (see Figure 7.4).

Figure 7.4 Sensory Behaviors: Seeking Smells and Tastes

Avoiding Smells and Tastes

Aversions to food based on smell and taste may play an important part in food selectivity. Otherwise, the same type of hypersensitivity described for other senses is reported for ASD. Sometimes it seems associated with particular smells (or tastes), for example, and other times a general sensitivity is present.

Sensory Behaviors Associated with Vision

Seeking Visual Experiences

There are a large number of behaviors associated with children seeking and creating visual experiences that appear to be of special interest to them and self-stimulating. These are covered in the previous chapter as well. The first type is those that the child can create himself by moving his head or body around, watching the visual effects created when he spins himself around or twirls on a tire swing, moving his hands or fingers in front of his face, or watching himself move in front of a mirror or other reflective surface. A second type is that which a child creates himself using objects, such as by dropping objects and watching them spin, moving or dangling strings or objects on strings, spinning the wheels on toy cars, or closely watching the wheels of toy vehicles while moving them across the floor or a surface. A third type is when the child finds the visual interests already occurring in the environment and spends a lot of time watching them: spinning fans, light reflecting off an object, cars moving past the front window, lights and letters and spinning wheels on TV game shows, and light and visual patterns on the computer screen (see Figure 7.5).

Avoiding Visual Experiences

Parents and others report that some children have a hard time with certain types of lights—for example, flickering fluorescents—and find them aversive, giving rise to upset behavior. Sensory hypersensitivity, while not exclusive to autism, does seem to arise in those with ASD so that things that are at a level comfortable for most people are too bright or too loud for children on the spectrum.

Wiggling fingers in front of eyes

Shaking head for visual effects

Visual interest while moving

Making things spin to watch them

Making things flap and wave to
watch them

Figure 7.5 Sensory Behaviors: Seeking Visual Experience

Sifting things (wood chips, beans) through fingers to watch them fall

Finding visual interests in the environment

Figure 7.5 Sensory Behaviors: Seeking Visual Experience *cont.*

Sensory Behaviors Associated with Sound

Seeking Sound Experiences

Some children are drawn very much to music, and seem to be able to develop a musical vocabulary much more easily than a spoken one. A more self-stimulatory activity is when the child makes sounds herself in a repetitive way, sounds that are not used in a communicative way, but because the child likes to hear them. They may be high-pitched, squeals, or growls, or they may be repetitive babbling or words or phrases said over and over again.

Avoiding Sound

Sound aversion issues for children on the spectrum tend to be of two different types. The first springs from a general sensitivity to sound and loud noises—such as vacuum cleaners or garage doors closing—that cause a very strong fear reaction. A related problem involves noisy places where there are a lot of activities—shopping malls, grocery stores, birthday parties, free play. The second type is aversion to specific sounds, which may not be that loud (e.g. bathroom vent fan) and may actually be quite soft. In this case, it would seem that the child reacts to a specific pitch or frequency as though it is highly irritating or overstimulating (see Figure 7.6). Some older children become specifically averse to human sounds, such as coughing, sneezing, throat-clearing, or chewing sounds.

Child finds noisy places and events stressful

Child finds certain noises aversive

Figure 7.6 Sensory Behaviors: Avoiding Sound

Highly Inconsistent Responses to Sound

Noteworthy in some children is the inconsistency in their response to sounds and language. Frequently, one of the first concerns parents have is that their child may have a hearing problem because he doesn't turn to his name being called, and may ignore loud sounds close to him. On the other hand, a child may hear the Barney theme song from the room farthest away from the TV, and come running to see his favorite character. Or he may hear the sound of the microwave beeping while he is in the backyard. It seems that the child is tuned into his own unique set of sounds, and ignores the rest.

Learning to Observe

Sensory sensitivities associated with movement, touch, and vision are the easiest ones to observe during an observation or assessment with a child. However, only a caregiver who is with the child continuously will be able to report thoroughly on them, and especially on issues with smell and taste.

Summary

Many clinicians think that a number of repetitive behaviors are in response to sensory-processing differences that result in a child either seeking extra input in one sense or another, or avoiding input that is unpleasant or overstimulating. Besides repetitive behaviors, however, some children with ASD show either great interest or great upset to sensory experiences across movement, touch, taste, smell, vision, and sound (see Table 7.1 for a summary).

Table 7.1 Sensory Behaviors Seen in Young Children with ASD

Sense	Movement	Touch	Smell and Taste	Vision	Hearing
Seeking	• High activity level • Running • Jumping • Spinning • Swinging • Rides, slides	• Seeks deep pressure (hugs, rubs head and self against furniture, floor) • Explores textures in unusual way with hands, body	• Seeks out smells in unusual way • Licks and tastes nonfood objects	• Seeks or creates visual experiences as described in Chapter 6	• Creates auditory environment using own vocalizations • Very attracted to music
Avoiding	• Low activity level • Avoids swinging, etc. • Stays close to ground	• Avoids light touches • Overreacts to unexpected or uncontrolled touches • "Tactile sensitive" to clothing, tags, hair brushing, food textures	• Hypersensitive to certain taste and smells and avoids them	• Avoids certain light levels and situations	• Hypersensitive to certain sounds and pitches • Avoids or overreacts to certain loud or sudden noises

Assessment of Young Children with, or Suspected to Have, Autism Spectrum Disorder

An Overview

This book has presented a detailed and systematic consideration of behaviors to observe as they may be related to ASD in very young children. The logical next step is to consider how these observations are brought together in the context of a professional evaluation, so that intervention services may proceed, if so indicated. A thorough treatment of this subject is beyond the scope of this current work, but an overview of the issues and strategies involved is offered as follows.

The Many Contexts of Early Childhood Assessment

There are many different settings in which a more formal or complete evaluation of a young child can occur. There is no single "ideal" approach, because the nature of the approach needs to match the assessment context for the child at the time of the referral. For example, the more thorough and extensive an evaluation is (e.g. involving multiple disciplines and multiple sessions), the longer it takes to accomplish, yet the child may benefit the most from entering into a program of intervention services as soon as possible. On the other hand, if a system allows for a quick entry into services through a single assessment session, the child may start treatment with important diagnostic questions unanswered—questions that may make a difference in how intervention is conducted.

Different professionals who have built up an expertise in ASD and developmental disabilities offer evaluations and consultations for the key issues and diagnosis: pediatric neurologists, child psychiatrists, developmental pediatricians, and child psychologists will see a child with the parent once or twice and give a diagnosis, then may or may not recommend further follow-up evaluations in medical fields (genetics, neurology, nutrition) and in developmental areas (speech-language, feeding, occupational and physical therapy). If a family lives near a university-based diagnostic assessment clinic, they may have access to a coordinated, multidisciplinary evaluation clinic with many experts. Other times, the family going through the public early intervention system may have a one-time, home-based team evaluation of two or more disciplines, although the assessing professionals may not have the capacity to offer an official diagnosis. They may or may not refer the family to a local MD or psychologist who can do so.

Geographic and regional differences play a very large role in what assessment and treatment resources are available to parents. Large metropolitan areas and their surrounding suburbs are, obviously, more resource-rich. As one travels further away from the city, resources become scarcer. In a semi-rural area, there may be one developmental pediatric office that has to handle all the referrals for miles around, and the resulting waiting list creates a barrier to quick action.

Given the rising number of autism cases that prevalence studies estimate, it will be important to find assessment solutions that balance a quick response with adequate evaluation practices. However, there are general guidelines that apply to almost every evaluation, and the rest of this chapter outlines them.

The Best Assessment Starts with Familiarity with Early Development and with a Broad Variety of Early Childhood Disorders

No state-of-the-art instrument or elaborate protocol can substitute for knowing what you are looking for and what constitutes typical development and thus departures from it. Early-career professionals, however, need to rely on solid, broad-based foundational training, then specialty training, good clinical supervision, and study until this knowledge becomes internalized. As well, working with infants, toddlers, and preschoolers requires direct training experience with this age group, as it is sufficiently different from working with older children.

There is a lot of interest currently in working with children with autism, but autism spectrum disorders need to be viewed within the larger context of developmental disabilities for several important reasons. First of all, almost all individual autism symptoms are shared by other disabilities, as well as with social-emotional disturbances. Clearly, differential diagnostic assessment entails knowing what other conditions may account for the presenting pictures of delays and differences. In addition, autism can be diagnosed along with other known genetic disorders (e.g. Fragile X) and medical problems (e.g. seizures) and can be accompanied by other developmental conditions, such as cognitive delay, low muscle tone, and coordination disorders. Some of the communication challenges in ASD are just the same as children with non-ASD language delays. Attentional difficulties seen in ASD can be shared with children with attention deficit hyperactivity disorder (ADHD) (or the child with ASD can have ADHD), and thus behavioral management is similar in this regard. There are myriad other examples of shared issues across different disabilities.

Second, so many of the assessment, consultation, management, treatment, educational, and policy issues germane to ASD are the same for disabilities in general. They are not specific to autism. While each different disability has its own unique features related to etiology, prevention, detection, assessment, treatment, and advocacy, the general contexts are not unique. The important issues that underlie carrying out assessments, collaborating with parents, linking assessment to intervention, conducting evidence-based research, developing and partnering with community programs, and networking with local, regional, and state programs are shared by most disabilities. Therefore, the autism specialist ideally needs at least to begin as a disabilities specialist, while developing a focus on ASD. Or else, if a focused interest in autism has led the professional into the field, it will be important to branch out somewhat to become familiar with a number of pediatric disabilities.

Assessment with Infants, Toddlers, and Preschoolers Has Its Unique Demands

Working with very young children requires significant flexibility in the approach to the child and in choosing assessment strategies and instruments. When learning to give tests and measurements to school-age children, standardization of administration (and thus validity) is predicated on the child being in an adequate state (alert, healthy, focused) to cooperate and perform. Yet, the younger the child is, the more changeable, and less controllable, his state (attentive and engaged vs. distracted or self-directed) and the less predictable his cooperation.

He cannot report on suboptimal states related to being tired, an illness beginning, or reluctance based on the particular activity or how it is being presented. As well, an older child has had more experiences in responding to the instructions of an adult other than his parent, and it is age-appropriate to do so, whereas the younger child cannot be expected to acclimatize as easily to a novel adult and novel tasks.

The evaluator thus needs the particular skills to work with young children and to adjust the pace, demands, and strategies to fit their temperaments and variable responses. Although there are many standardized instruments of ability across different domains (cognitive, language, motor, adaptive) for infants and toddlers, the practitioner working with very young children, and especially those with disabilities, needs a wide repertoire of instruments and strategies, including non-standardized approaches. (Non-standardized refers to criterion-referenced instruments and play-based approaches.) A range of options is called for because of both the great variability in information-processing abilities of children with disabilities and the extent to which some children are simply not well suited for standardized instruments.

In addition, the professional in this field needs skills to work with a young child and her caregivers together. The next section discusses the related topic of partnering with caregivers during assessment.

Family-centered Practice Shapes Assessment Strategies in Highly Specific Ways

Best-practice guidelines for early intervention and its components, including evaluation and assessment, include family-centered strategies (Dempsey & Keen, 2008). This principle incorporates the notion that families should have the opportunity to be full partners in early intervention activities, for a wide variety of reasons. The most fundamental rationale is that caregivers—not the professionals—are the constant in their child's life over time, and thus their interface with professionals needs to support their growth as advocates as much as it supports a child's development.

Parent-as-advocate does not have a single face, but instead adapts according to the caregiver's concerns, resources, strengths, and challenges. The most effective parent–professional partnership is a dynamic process where the expertise and goals of the parent meet those of the professional in a way that keeps building decision-making ability in the parent, regardless of the level it has started out.

As regards assessment, then, the evaluator has the opportunity to involve the caregiver such that he gains both knowledge and confidence as a result of going through the evaluation. This knowledge relates to understanding the assessment process itself, gaining familiarity with tests and measurements, and of course learning about the nature of his child's functioning, strengths, and needs. Then, directly linked to the assessment process is the recommended intervention, around which the parent also learns about the service system, advocating within it, and anticipating next steps.

What are the ways that evaluators can conduct family-centered assessments for young children with or at risk for ASD? Table 8.1 outlines some basic strategies.

There is no doubt that an evaluation aimed at determining the presence of autism spectrum disorder can present a time of great stress and upset for caregivers. To establish a collaborative partnership during the assessment, wherein an authentic give-and-take occurs, helps to transfer a sense of greater control to the parent and can mitigate somewhat the trauma of hearing difficult news. In addition, the professional involved in early childhood assessment needs to have received training in communicating difficult information to parents.

General Choices for Assessment Strategies

At the start of the chapter, it was emphasized that assessment and evaluation contexts can vary significantly. The clinician usually finds herself in a setting wherein many parameters have already been set. Nonetheless, providers need to think critically about choices that can be made to optimize meeting the goals of the assessment according to best-practice principles in early intervention. For example, Table 8.1 showed ways in which the usual procedures are "tweaked" in a way to produce a more family-centered result. In the same way, each feature of the evaluation planning and implementation can incorporate choices that make the evaluation more effective given the presenting referral.

One helpful distinction is the assessment strategy versus the assessment battery. The strategy involves the actual approach with respect to how many people are involved, how the assessment is carried out over time, and whether the evaluators adopt a more standardized, play-based, or functional approach (or a combination of these). The assessment battery refers to the chosen instruments, which will tend to vary based on the strategy the clinicians will be using.

Table 8.1 Family-centered Assessment Compared
with Traditional Assessment

Family-centered	Traditional
Pre-assessment planning takes place. Conversations between parents and evaluators ahead of time establish that this is a collaborative effort.	Administrative assistant makes appointment and parents are told when and where to show up.
Pre-assessment conversations give the parent the opportunity to voice her concerns about her child and their goals for the evaluation in her own words, and this information is incorporated into the assessment goals and procedures.	Referral information is standardized and/or from another professional source. Assessment goals proceed from a standardized evaluation protocol.
Pre-assessment conversations give parents choices, to the extent possible, about when and where the evaluation may take place and who can be there (parent may not realize he can have spouse, mother, friend, babysitter present).	Evaluation place and participants are dictated by the agency.
Pre-assessment conversations give the parent a preview of what will occur during the evaluation, in order to reduce trepidation that may be present in part by not knowing what will happen.	Parent is not walked through, ahead of time, how the evaluation will proceed.
The child and parent are kept together during the assessment.	The parent is separated from the child or watches behind a one-way mirror.
The evaluation is narrated by the professional (or another provider) while it is occurring, explaining what is being done, what information it may yield, and what some of the observations are.	The assessment is conducted without informing the parent what the procedures are and what type of information they yield.
The evaluation fully incorporates observations from the parent and parent-report instruments; the clinician is trained to ultimately determine the veridicality of the report.	Parent-report is minimally incorporated.
Feedback (at least preliminary) is given at the end of the assessment. The parent anticipates written reports that mirror what has been discussed to date.	Parent is told to wait till all procedures and further assessments are completed before results can be discussed.
Evaluation reports are written in strength-based, understandable language and are discussed with parents.	Evaluation reports are written so that only other professionals can understand them.

There are pros and cons for each of the major strategies. Multidisciplinary evaluations that extend over several weeks give the optimal opportunity to collect many behavioral samples from the child, and thus increase the reliability of the observations. Parents also benefit from the time and from repeated interactions with professionals in order to understand their child's issues, give their own perspective, and start to integrate internally what different scenarios may occur as a result of the evaluation. Some of the downsides of this approach involve the time it takes, the expense of these procedures, and the likelihood that the parent has to give redundant information and the child has to repeat the same tasks for different professionals.

What about where the child is seen? There are pros and cons for clinic vs. home-based settings as well. Many experts seeing young children in the home favor that setting because the child is the most comfortable there and some of the issues of best performance eroded by unfamiliar settings are obviated. On the other hand, the home setting has a lot of unpredictable features that can challenge the reliability of the procedures. Choosing the setting can be addressed in the pre-assessment planning process reflected in Table 8.1.

Another distinction that is made in early childhood evaluation approaches is whether an arena assessment is performed or individual evaluations take place. Arena assessments are where two or more professionals are present and each conducts their evaluations over a single session, although one person may take the lead and interact more than the others with the child. Arena assessments have the advantage of efficiency in terms of time and information exchange, but they do require specific training and experience on the part of the professionals.

A final parameter is whether a play-based, curriculum-based/ criterion referenced, or standardized instrument approach is taken, or some combination of these. These approaches arrange themselves on a continuum of how constrained the examiner is in terms of task administration and materials used, even though each approach attempts to evaluate basically the same constructs. As with the other parameters discussed, there are advantages and disadvantages for each approach. The professional evaluator working with young children with disabilities and their families benefits from having options for consideration of individual children and their caregivers as well as the given assessment goals.

Choices for Assessment Instruments for ASD in Young Children

One of the fundamental tenets of abilities assessment is that data are gathered from more than one source, and ideally from at least three—direct interaction with the child yielding clinical observations; standardized assessment using standardized tasks, administration, and scoring; and information from a caregiver or teacher who has known the child for an extended period of time (Meyer *et al.*, 2001; Reynolds, Livingston, & Willson, 2008).

There are a number of examples of developmental assessment instruments that accommodate each of these information-gathering perspectives, but this section is limited to tools specifically for ASD.

Parent- and Teacher-Report Instruments

These tools have important advantages. The parents or caregivers have a level of familiarity with their child's behavior that cannot be replaced by anyone else. Additionally, these procedures give scores and results regardless of how problematic it is to examine the child extensively. Studies have shown that in general parents are reliable reporters (Dale, 1991; Eiser & Morse, 2001; Waschbusch, Daleiden, & Drabman, 2000). Nonetheless, there are circumstances where the parent may not be a reliable reporter, and the evaluator must make a decision about whether the test or procedure used was a reliable one.

The results of a caregiver-rated instrument would be combined with other ways of gathering information, such as tasks administered directly to the child and clinical observations. Thus, parent-report is one piece of a larger picture compiled to reach diagnostic decisions.

AUTISM SPECTRUM RATING SCALES

The Autism Spectrum Rating Scales (Goldstein & Naglieri, 2010) are a caregiver-rated instrument with separate forms for ages 2 to 5 years and 6 to 18 years. In addition, there is a teacher-rated form. The focus here is on the parent-rated form for ages 2 to 5 years, for which there is a short form (15 items) and a longer one (70). The longer form takes about 20 minutes for the caregiver to complete. Each item is rated using a five-point Likert rating format to reflect how often each behavior is observed. The main scales reflect current DSM diagnostic criteria— Social/Communication and Unusual Behaviors—and a Total Score that unifies them. There is a "DSM-IV-TR" scale that uses items most closely matched to specific DSM criteria. There are eight other subscales referred to as Treatment Scales that evaluate Peer Socialization, Social/Emotional Reciprocity, Atypical Language, Behavioral Rigidity, and other areas. All scales have a mean of 50 and a standard deviation (SD) of 10 (T scores). One SD above or below the mean is considered within the "Average" range, while 1½ SDs is "Slightly Elevated," between 1½ and 2 SDs "Elevated," and over 2 SDs "Very Elevated."

INFANT-TODDLER CHECKLIST

The Infant-Toddler Checklist is part of the Communication and Symbolic Behavior Scales—Developmental Profile (Wetherby & Prizant, 2002). For children with functional communication skills ranging from 6 months to 24 months (and up to 72 months chronologically for children with frank delays), this caregiver-rated scale functions both as a screening instrument and as a measurement instrument in the context of a more complete evaluation. For a screener, it can be downloaded from the Internet along with scoring guidelines that provide age-based cut-off scores ("Of Concern" or "No Concern"). With the purchase of a manual, standardized scores can be obtained using the same form. There are 14 total items, and subscales consist of Emotion and Eye Gaze, Communication, Gestures, Sounds, Words, Understanding, and Object Use. These are collapsed to three final scales of Social, Speech, and Symbolic Composites, the standard scores for which have a mean of 10 and a standard deviation of 3. These are further collapsed into a Total Score, which has a mean of 100 and SD of 15. While this and the tool below are not intended to be used alone for an ASD diagnosis, it does report out on very relevant symptoms for especially young children, and has been shown to predict ASD in recent studies (Pierce *et al.*, 2011).

CAREGIVER QUESTIONNAIRE

The Caregiver Questionnaire is also part of the Communication and Symbolic Behavior Scales—Developmental Profile (Wetherby & Prizant, 2002). This questionnaire is an expanded version of the above, consisting of 41 items. There are four additional open-ended questions about communication and other concerns, as well as about the child's strengths. It also is to be completed by a primary caregiver for a child, and covers the same ages. It yields standardized scores for the same subscales and scales of the Infant-Toddler Checklist.

INFANT TODDLER SOCIAL EMOTIONAL ASSESSMENT

The Infant Toddler Social Emotional Assessment (ITSEA: Carter & Briggs-Gowan, 2000) is a parent-rated instrument and spanning the ages 12 to 36 months. Although it is a broader behavioral assessment, it has a number of items that are specific to ASD. The Parent form is rather long (166 items), taking 25–30 minutes to complete. It yields the following four broad domain scores: Externalizing, Internalizing, Dysregulation, and Competence. Each of these domains has subscales such as Activity/Impulsivity, Aggression/Defiance, General Anxiety, Separation Distress, Sleep, Eating, Negative Emotionality, Compliance, and Attention; there are 17 subscales in all. The subscales that may show sensitivity to ASD include Dysregulation, Sensory Sensitivities, Empathy, and Pro-social Peer Relations. There is a teacher-rated form that does not have standardized scoring. A shorter form of the ITSEA is the BITSEA (Brief Infant-Toddler Social-Emotional Assessment; Briggs-Gowan & Carter, 2001), but it is not as sensitive to ASD issues.

TEMPERAMENT AND ATYPICAL BEHAVIOR SCALE

The Temperament and Atypical Behavior Scale (Bagnato, Neisworth, Salvia, & Hunt, 1999) is a parent-rated questionnaire for children ages 11 to 71 months. There are two versions, a 15-item Screener and 55-item Assessment Tool. It is not explicitly for diagnosis of ASD, but it does yield important behavioral information relevant to the diagnosis, with items relevant to revealing self-regulation problems in the temperament, sensory, and social realm. The Assessment Tool has four subscales: Detached, Hypersensitive-active, Underreactive and Dysregulated, and a Total Score, each with a mean of 50 and SD of 10 (T scores).

Parent Interview Instruments

A detailed, clinical interview with a caregiver who is highly familiar with the child as well as a reliable reporter is a cornerstone of any early childhood evaluation. This person is relied upon for medical and developmental history as well as all features of current functioning; the caregiver also helps to determine the level of distress or concern the child's behavior is causing. The following instrument, however, was created to address autism spectrum symptoms specifically and is widely used in research.

AUTISM DIAGNOSTIC INTERVIEW-REVISED

The Autism Diagnostic Interview-Revised (ADI-R: Rutter, LeCouteur, & Lord, 2003) is an extensive interview (taking 1½ to 2½ hours) consisting of 93 questions administered to a caregiver. There are three domains of questions—Language/Communication, Reciprocal Social Interaction, and Restricted, Repetitive, and Stereotyped Behaviors and Interests. Summary scores are derived from the scoring protocol in the areas of Communication, Reciprocal Social Interaction, Repetitive Behaviors, and to what degree symptoms are reported from below four to five years of age.

In recent years there have been attempts to adapt the scoring of the ADI-R, as well as the relative scoring of the ADOS (see below) and the ADI-R, so that it is more useful for toddlers younger than two years of age (Wiggins & Robins, 2008).

Clinician-Rated Instruments

The following instrument stands alone as a clinician-rated, judgment-based instrument. The judgment-based method differs from that of a checklist because each behavior is judged on a continuum from normal to abnormal. The judgment itself is guided by written behavioral anchors for each level, as well as by the experienced clinician's judgment after interacting with the child for an extended period.

CHILDHOOD AUTISM RATING SCALE, 2ND EDITION

The Childhood Autism Rating Scale, 2nd Edition (CARS-2: Schopler, Van Bourgondien, Wellman, & Love, 2010) is a standardized, 15-item scale that is filled out by a clinician after spending time with the child that usually involves test administration and clinical observation. It spans the ages 2 to adult, with separate norms for children 2 to 12 years vs. 12 years to adulthood. The CARS-2 also has a High-Functioning Form, as contrasted to its Standard Form. Whereas the judgment scorings for the Standard Form are based on direct observations of the evaluator, the High-Functioning form allows for information gathered from teachers and parents.

Only the Standard Form is used with very young children. The items include such behavioral clusters as Relating to People, Object Use, Body Use, Verbal and Nonverbal Communication, Intellectual Functioning Level, and a General Impressions items. Each item is rated from 0 (for no abnormality) to 4 (severe abnormality), with the opportunity to score between whole numbers (e.g. 2.5). The total raw score is obtained by summing the score for all 15 items; level of symptomatology is then expressed both along a continuum of severity and as a standard score. The continuum score designates that scores in the interval of 15–29 represent "Minimal to No Symptoms of Autism Spectrum Disorders"; from 30 to 36.5 represent "Mild to Moderate Symptoms of Autism Spectrum Disorders"; and 37+ represent "Severe Symptoms of Autism Spectrum Disorders." The standard scoring system represents a different approach. Using a mean of 50 and an SD of 10 (T scores), this score shows the level of autism symptoms compared to *other* children or individuals also on the spectrum.

Structured Observation Instruments
AUTISM DIAGNOSTIC OBSERVATION SCALE

The Autism Diagnostic Observation Scale (ADOS: Lord, Rutter, DiLavore, & Risi, 2001) was a breakthrough instrument that now has become a standard for research measurement. It is a semi-structured interactive observation protocol that sets up situations for the child or adult to demonstrate the features of autism. The ADOS requires training from a qualified practitioner, with a start-up workshop of two days. To assure reliability on research projects, the training is more extensive and reliability checks are ongoing.

One of the most important features of the ADOS is choosing the correct module, based on verbal ability, for the individual being evaluated. Module 1, which is geared for those without phrase speech, is to be used both with toddlers and preschoolers *and* older children with severe language delays. Module 2, for those with phrase speech but not fluent language, would be used with a variety of ages as well. The second innovation of the ADOS is the scoring algorithms. Raw scores are obtained across subscales, and different cut-off levels are specified for different subscales, so that the specification of ASD is based on a profile rather than an omnibus score. In research development of the ADOS, adjusting the cut-off scores for the different subscales results in greater or less inclusion agreement with other classification strategies, such as clinical diagnosis.

To accurately score the ADOS, the examiner also needs to be familiar with typical and atypical development, and with autism behavior in particular. For example, repetitive speech or behavior can occur anytime during the interaction, and the examiner has to be able to recognize and note it, even though it can be subtle to the uninitiated.

The ADOS-2 (Lord *et al.*, 2012) has therefore been informed by over a decade of research, and has revised algorithm and comparison scores for Modules 1 through 3. The addition of a Toddler Module (Lord, Luyster, Gotham, & Guthrie, 2012) is very important as well, because it is over the last decade that clinicians and researchers have been focusing on early identification.

SCREENING TEST FOR AUTISM IN TODDLERS

The Screening Test for Autism in Toddlers (STAT: Stone & Ousley, 2006; see also Stone, Coonrod, Turner, & Pozdol, 2004) is a Level 2 screening instrument based on structured play interactions. "Level 2" means that a child has already been identified as being at risk for having a developmental disability, but the nature of the problem has not been specified further. Therefore, Level 2 instruments are specific to screen for autism, but not comprehensive diagnostic measures.

The STAT takes approximately 20 minutes to administer and consists of 12 tasks that address the child's abilities in the areas of imitation, play, requesting, and directing attention, among others. It targets behaviors that research has shown to represent core symptoms in two-year-olds. As it is a screener, it yields cut-off scores signifying risk vs. no risk. Training for the STAT can now be done online through Vanderbilt University.

Summary

Evaluators benefit from having foundational knowledge about early development and about early childhood disabilities in general as they gain familiarity with ASD in particular. Specific training for, and experience with, very young children is needed in order to work with this specialized population, training that includes how to conduct services in a family-centered way. There are a number of strategies to choose from with respect to how assessments are carried out, for example choosing where they take place and how the professional disciplines work together. In addition, there are a number of types of autism-specific instruments to choose from for very young children.

References

Bagnato, S. J., Neisworth, J. T., Salvia, J. J., & Hunt, F. M. (1999). *Temperament and Atypical Behavior Scale (TABS): Early childhood indicators of developmental dysfunction.* Baltimore, MD: Paul H. Brookes.

Ben-Sasson, A., Cermak, S. A., Orsmond, G. I., Tager-Flusberg, H. T., Carter, A., Kadlec, M. B., *et al.* (2007). Extreme sensory modulation behaviors in toddlers with autism spectrum disorders. *American Journal of Occupational Therapy, 61*(5), 584–592.

Boyd, B. A., Baraneck, G. T., Sideris, J., Poe, M. D., Watson, L. R., Patten, E., *et al.* (2010). Sensory features and repetitive behaviors in children with autism and developmental delays. *Autism Research, 3*(2), 78–87.

Briggs-Gowan, M, & Carter, A. (2001). *Brief Infant Toddler Social Emotional Assessment.* San Antonio, TX: Pearson.

Camras, L. A., & Fatani, S. S. (2008). The development of facial expressions. In M. Lewis, J. M. Haviland-Jones, & L. F. Barrett (Eds.), *Handbook of emotions* (3rd ed.). New York: Guilford Press.

Carter, A., & Briggs-Gowan, M. (2000). *Infant Toddler Social Emotional Assessment.* San Antonio, TX: Pearson.

Coonrod, E. E., & Stone, W. L. (2004). Early concerns of parents with autistic and nonautistic disorders. *Infants and Young Children, 17*(3), 258–268.

Dale, P. S. (1991). The validity of a parent report measure of vocabulary and syntax at 24 months. *Journal of Speech and Hearing Research, 34,* 565–571.

Dempsey, I., & Keen, D. (2008). A review of processes and outcomes in family-centered services for children with a disability. *Topics in Early Childhood Special Education, 28*(1), 42–52.

Dominick, K. C., Davis, N. O., Lainhart, J., Tager-Flusberg, H., & Folstein, S. (2007). Atypical behaviors in children with autism and children with a history of language impairment. *Research in Developmental Disabilities, 28*(2), 145–162.

Eiser, R., & Morse, R. (2001). Can parents rate their child's health-related quality of life? Results of a systematic review. *Quality of Life Research, 10*(4), 347–357.

Falck-Ytter, T., & von Hofsten, C. (2011). How special is social looking in ASD: A review. *Progress in Brain Research, 189,* 209–222.

Fitzer, A., & Sturmey, P. (2009). *Language and autism: Applied behavior analysis, evidence, and practice.* Austin, TX: Pro-Ed.

Goldstein, S., & Naglieri, J. A. (2010). *Autism Spectrum Rating Scales.* Toronto: Multi-Health Systems.

Hebbeler, K., Spiker, D., Mallik, S., Scarborough, A., & Simeonsson, R. (2003). *Demographic characteristics of children and families entering early intervention.* [NEILS Data Report No. 3.] Menlo Park, CA: SRI International.

Kim, S. H., & Lord, C. (2010). Restricted and repetitive behaviors in toddlers and preschoolers with autism spectrum disorders based on the Autism Diagnostic Observation Schedule (ADOS). *Autism Research, 3*(4), 162–173.

Klin, A., & Volkmar, F. R. (2003). Asperger syndrome: Diagnosis and external validity. *Child and Adolescent Psychiatry Clinics of North America, 12*(1), 1–13.

Koegel, R. L., Bharoocha, A. A., Ribnick, C. B., Ribnick, R. C., Bucio, M. O., Fredeen, R. M., *et al.* (2011). Using individualized reinforcers and hierarchical exposure to increase food flexibility in children with autism spectrum disorders. *Journal of Autism and Developmental Disorders, 42*(8), 1574–1581.

Lam, K. S. L., Bodfish, J. W., & Piven, J. (2008). Evidence for three subtypes of repetitive behavior in autism that differ in familiality and association with other symptoms. *Journal of Child Psychology and Psychiatry, 49*(11), 1193–1200.

Lord, C., Luyster, R. J., Gotham, K., & Guthrie, W. (2012). *ADOS-2 Toddler Module.* Torrance, CA: Western Psychological Services.

Lord, C., Rutter, M., DiLavore, P. C., & Risi, S. (2001). *Autism Diagnostic Observation Scale.* Torrance, CA: Western Psychological Services.

Lord, C., Rutter, M., DiLavore, P. C., Risi, S., Gotham, K., & Bishop, S. (2012). *Autism Diagnostic Observation Scale-2.* Torrance, CA: Western Psychological Services.

Mandell, D. S., Novak, M. A., & Zubritsky, C. D. (2005). Factors associated with age of diagnosis among children with autism spectrum disorders. *Pediatrics, 116*(6), 1480–1486.

Meyer, G. J., Finn, S. E., Eyde, L. D., Kay, G. G., Moreland, K. L., Dies, R. R., *et al.* (2001). Psychological testing and psychologist assessment: A review of evidence and issues. *American Psychologist, 56*(2), 128–165.

Mondloch, C. J., Lewis, T. L., Budreau, D. R., Maurer, D., Dannemiller, J. L., Stephens, B. R., *et al.* (1999). *Psychological Science, 10*(5), 419–422.

Mooney, E. L., Gray, K. M., Tonge, B. J., Sweeney, D. J., & Taffe, J. R. (2009). Factor analytic study of repetitive behaviors in young children with pervasive developmental disorders. *Journal of Autism and Developmental Disorders, 39,* 765–774.

Pierce, K., Carter, C., Weinfeld, M., Desmond, J., Hazin, R., Bjork, R., *et al.* (2011). Detecting, studying, and treating autism early: The one-year well-baby check-up approach. *Journal of Pediatrics, 159*(3), 458–465.

Reynolds, C. R., Livingston, R. B., & Willson, V. (2008). *Measurement and assessment in education* (2nd ed.). Boston, MA: Pearson.

Richler, J., Hierta, M., Bishop, S. L., & Lord, C. (2010). Developmental trajectories of restricted and repetitive behaviors and interests in children with autism spectrum disorders. *Development and Psychopathology, 22,* 55–69.

Rogers, S. J. (2009). What are infant siblings teaching us about autism in infancy? *Autism Research, 2*(3), 125–137.

Rogers, S. J., Hepburn, S. L., Stackhouse, T., & Wehner, E. (2003). Imitation performance in toddlers with autism and those with other developmental disorders. *Journal of Child Psychology and Psychiatry, 44*(5), 763–781.

Rutter, M., LeCouteur, A., & Lord, C. (2003). *Autism Diagnostic Interview-Revised.* Torrance, CA: Western Psychological Services.

Saint-Georges, C., Cassel, R. S., Cohen, D., Chetouani, M., Laznick, M., Maestro, S., *et al.* (2010). What studies of family home movies can teach us about autistic infants: A literature review. *Research in Autism Spectrum Disorders, 4*(3), 355–366.

Schopler, E., Van Bourgondien, M. E., Wellman, G. J., & Love, S. (2010). *Childhood Autism Rating Scale, 2nd Edition (CARS2).* Torrance, CA: Western Psychological Services.

Stone, W. L., Coonrod, E. E., Turner, L. M., & Pozdol, S. L. (2004). Psychometric properties of the STAT for early autism screening. *Journal of Autism and Developmental Disorders, 34*(6), 691–701.

Stone, W., & Ousley, O. (2006). *Screening Test for Autism in Toddlers.* Nashville, TN: Vanderbilt University.

Striano, T., & Rochat, P. (2000). Emergence of selective referencing in infancy. *Infancy, 1*(2), 253–264.

Tomasello, N. M., Manning, A. R., & Dulmus, C. N. (2010). Family-centered early intervention for infants and toddlers with disabilities. *Journal of Family Social Work, 13*(2), 163–172.

Tronick, E. (2007). *The neurobehavioral and social-emotional development of infants and children* (Norton Series on Interpersonal Neurobiology). New York: W. W. Norton & Company.

Turati, C., Simion, F., Milani, I., & Umilta, C. (2002). Newborns' preference for faces. *Developmental Psychology, 38*(6), 875–882.

Turner, M. A. (1997). Towards an executive dysfunction account of repetitive behavior in autism. In J. Russell (Ed.), *Autism as an executive disorder.* Oxford: Oxford University Press.

Turner, M. A. (1999). Annotation: Repetitive behavior in autism: A review of psychological research. *Journal of Child Psychiatry, 40*(6), 839–849.

Walker, D. R., Thompson, A., Zwaigenbaum, L., Goldberg, J., Bryson, S. E., Mahoney, W. J., *et al.* (2004). Specifying PDD-NOS: A comparison of PDD-NOS, Asperger syndrome, and autism. *Journal of the American Academy of Child and Adolescent Psychiatry, 43*(2), 172–180.

Waschbusch, D. A., Daleiden, E., & Drabman, R. S. (2000). Are parents accurate reporters of their child's cognitive abilities? *Journal of Psychopathology and Behavioral Assessment, 22*(1), 61–77.

Wetherby, A. M., & Prizant, B. M. (2002). *Communication and Symbolic Behavior Scales-DP: Caregiver Questionnaire.* Baltimore: Paul H. Brookes Publishing Company.

Wetherby, A. M., & Prizant, B. M. (2002). *Communication and Symbolic Behavior Scales-DP: Infant-Toddler Checklist.* Baltimore: Paul H. Brookes Publishing Company.

Wiggins, L., & Robins, D. L. (2008). Brief report: Excluding the ADI-R behavioral domain improves diagnostic agreement in toddlers. *Journal of Autism and Developmental Disorders, 38*(5), 972–976.

Further Reading

Early Intervention and ASD

Boyd, B. A., Odom, S. L., Humphreys, B. P., & Sam, A. M. (2010). Infants and toddlers with autism spectrum disorder: Early identification and early intervention. *Journal of Early Intervention, 32*(2), 75–98.

Dawson, G. (2008). Early behavioral intervention, brain plasticity, and the prevention of autism spectrum disorder. *Development and Psychopathology, 20*, 775–803.

Dawson, G., Rogers, S., Munson, J., Smith, M., Winter, J., Greenson, J., *et al.* (2009). Randomized, controlled trial of an intervention for toddlers with autism: The Early Start Denver Model. *Pediatrics, 125*(1), 17–23.

Eldevik, S., Hastings, R. P., Hughes, J. C., Jahr, E., Eikeseth, S., & Cross, S. (2009). Meta-analysis of early intensive behavioral intervention for children with autism. *Journal of Clinical Child and Adolescent Psychology, 38*(3), 439–450.

Strain, P. S., & Bovey, E. H. (2011). Randomized, controlled trial of the LEAP Model of early intervention for young children with autism spectrum disorders. *Topics in Early Childhood Special Education, 31*(3), 133–154.

Strain, P. S., Schwartz, I. S., & Barton, E. E. (2011). Providing interventions for young children with autism spectrum disorders: What we still need to accomplish. *Journal of Early Intervention, 33*(4), 321–332.

Baby Sibs Studies

Gamliel, I., Yirmiva, N., Jaffe, D. H., Manor, O., & Sigman, M. (2009). Developmental trajectories in siblings of children with autism: Cognition and language from 4 months to 7 years. *Journal of Autism and Developmental Disorders, 39*(8), 1131–1144.

Newschaffer, C. J., Croen, L., Fallin, M. D., Hertz-Picciotto, I., Nguyen, D. V., Lee, N. L., *et al.* (2012). Infant siblings and the investigation of autism risk factors. *Journal of Neurodevelopmental Disorders, 4*, 7.

Rogers, S. J. (2009). What are infant siblings teaching us about autism in infancy? *Autism Research, 2*(3), 125–137.

Studies of Very Early Differentiating Behavior

Eyler, L. T., Pierce, K., & Courchesne, E. (2012). A failure of left temporal cortex to specialize for language is an early emerging and fundamental property of autism. *Brain, 135*(3), 949–960.

McCleery, J. P., Akshoomoff, N., Dobkins, K. R., & Carver, L. J. (2009). Atypical face versus object processing and hemispheric asymmetries in 10-month-old infants at risk for autism. *Biologic Psychiatry, 66*(10), 950–957.

Ozonoff, S., Young, G. S., Goldring, S., Greiss-Hess, L., Herrera, A. M., Steele, J., *et al.* (2008). Gross motor development, movement abnormalities, and early identification of autism. *Journal of Autism and Developmental Disorders, 38*(4), 644–656.

Young, G. S., Merin, N., Rogers, S. J., & Ozonoff, S. (2009). Gaze behavior and affect at 6 months: Predicting clinical outcomes and language development in typically developing infants and infants at risk for autism. *Developmental Science, 12*(5), 798–814.

Intellectual Disability and ASD

Leonard, H., Glasson, E., Nassar, N., Whitehouse, T., Bebbington, A., Bourke, P., *et al.* (2011). Autism and intellectual disability are differentially related to sociodemographic background at birth. *PLoS One, 6*(3), e17875.

Matson, J. L., & Shoemaker, M. (2009). Intellectual disability and its relationship to autism spectrum disorders. *Research in Developmental Disabilities, 30,* 1107–1114.

Mefford, H. C., Batshaw, M. L., & Hoffman, E. P. (2012). Genomics, intellectual disability, and autism. *New England Journal of Medicine, 366,* 733–743.

Neuropsychological Profiles of ASD

Fein, D. (2011). *The neuropsychology of autism.* New York: Oxford University Press.

Comorbidities and ASD

Amiet, C., Gourfinkel-An, I., Bouzamondo, A., Tordjman. S., Baulac, M., Lechat, P., *et al.* (2008). Epilepsy in autism is associated with intellectual disability and gender: Evidence from a meta-analysis. *Biological Psychiatry, 64*(7), 577–582.

Dimitrios, I., Zafeiriou, D., Ververi, A., & Vargiami, E. (2007). Childhood autism and associated comorbidities. *Brain and Development, 29*(5), 257–272.

Mefford, H. C., Batshaw, M. L., & Hoffman, E. P. (2012). Genomics, intellectual disability, and autism. *New England Journal of Medicine, 366,* 733–743.

Feeding Problems and ASD

Emond, A., Emmett, P., Steer, C., & Golding, J. (2010). Feeding symptoms, dietary patterns, and growth in young children with autism spectrum disorders. *Pediatrics, 126*(2), 337–342.

Rogers, L. G., Magill-Evans, J., & Rempel, G. R. (2012). Mothers' challenges in feeding their children with autism spectrum disorder—Managing more than just picky eating. *Journal of Developmental and Physical Disabilities, 24*(1), 19–33.

Sleep Problems and ASD

Cotton, S. M., & Richdale, A. L. (2010). Sleep patterns and behaviour in typically developing children and children with autism, Down syndrome, Prader-Willi syndrome and intellectual disability. *Research in Autism Spectrum Disorders, 4*(3), 490–500.

Sivertsen, B., Posserud, M., Lundervold, A. J., & Hysing, M. (2012). Sleep problems in children with autism spectrum problems: A longitudinal population-based study. *Autism, 16,* 139–150.

Developmental Trajectories of ASD

Lord, C., Luyster, R., Guthrie, W., & Pickles, A. (2012). Patterns of developmental trajectories in toddlers with autism spectrum disorder. *Journal of Consulting and Clinical Psychology, 80*(3), 477–489.

Ozonoff, S., Iosif, A., Baguio, F., Cook, I. C., Hill, M. M., Hutman, T., *et al.* (2010). Prospective study of the emergence of early behavioral signs of autism. *Journal of the American Academy of Child and Adolescent Psychiatry, 49*(3), 256–266.

Typical Language Development

Owens, R. (2011). *Language development: An introduction* (8th ed.). New York: Allyn & Bacon.

Language Development in Young Children with ASD

Eigstia, I., Marchenaa, A. B., Schuha, J. M., & Kelley, E. (2011). Language acquisition in autism spectrum disorders: A developmental review. *Research in Autism Spectrum Disorders, 5*(2), 681–691.

Luyster, R. J., Kadlec, M. B., Carter, A., & Tager-Flusberg, H. (2008). Language assessment and development in toddlers with autism spectrum disorders. *Journal of Autism and Developmental Disorders, 38*(8), 1426–1438.

Rapin, I., Dunn, M. A., Allen, D., Stevens, M. C., & Fein, D. (2009). Subtypes of language disorders in school-age children with autism. *Developmental Neuropsychology, 34*(1), 66–84.

Rice, M. L., & Warren, S. F. (2005). Language symptoms of developmental language disorders: An overview of autism, Down syndrome, fragile X, specific language impairment, and Williams syndrome. *Applied Linguistics, 26*(1), 7–27.

Tager-Flusberg, H., & Caronna, E. (2007). Language disorders: Autism and other pervasive developmental disorders. *Pediatric Clinics of North America, 54*(3), 469–481.

Tager-Flusberg, H., Paul, R., & Lord, C. (2005). Language and communication in autism. In F. Volkmar, A. Klin, R. Paul, & D. Cohen (Eds.), *Handbook of autism and pervasive developmental disorders* (3rd ed.). New York: Wiley.

Wetherby, A., Watt, N., Morgan, L., & Shumway, S. (2011). Social communication profiles of children with autism spectrum disorders late in the second year of life. *Journal of Autism and Developmental Disorders, 37*(5), 960–975.

Assistive Technology and Augmentative Communication

Schlosser, R. W., & Wendt, O. (2008). Effects of augmentative and alternative communication intervention of speech production in children with autism: A systematic review. *American Journal of Speech-Language Pathology, 17,* 212–230.

General Social Development

Bornstein, M. H., Lamb, M. E., & Teti, D. M. (2002). *Development in infancy: An introduction* (4th ed.). Mahwah, NJ: Lawrence Erlbaum.

Tronick, E. (2007). *The neurobehavioral and social-emotional development of infants and children* (Norton Series on Interpersonal Neurobiology). New York: W. W. Norton & Company.

Eye Contact in Young Children with ASD

Kylliainen, A., Wallace, S., Coutanche, M. N., Leppanen, J. M., Cusack, J., Bailey, A. J., *et al.* (2012). Affective-motivational brain responses to direct gaze in children with autism spectrum disorder. *Journal of Child Psychology and Psychiatry, 53*(7), 790–797.

Senju, A., & Johnson, M. H. (2009). Atypical eye contact in autism: Models, mechanisms, and development. *Neuroscience and Biobehavioral Reviews, 33*(8), 1204–1214.

Imitation in ASD

Hamilton, A. F. (2008). Emulation and mimicry for social interaction: A theoretical approach to imitation in autism. *Quarterly Journal of Experimental Psychology, 61*(1), 101–115.

Rogers, S. (2006). Studies of imitation in early infancy: Findings and theories. In S. J. Rogers, & J. H. G. Williams (Eds.), *Imitation and the social mind: Autism and typical development.* New York: Guilford Press.

Sustained Social Interaction, Joint Attention, and Reciprocity

Dawson, G., Munson, J., Estes, A., Osterling, J., McPartland, J., Toth, K., *et al.* (2002). Neurocognitive function and joint attention ability in young children with autism spectrum disorder versus developmental delay. *Child Development, 73*(2), 345–358.

Dawson, G., Toth, K., Abbott, R., Osterling, J., Munson, J., Estes, A., *et al.* (2004). Early social attention impairments in autism: Social orienting, joint attention, and attention to distress. *Developmental Psychology, 40*(2), 271–283.

Eilan, N., Hoerl, C., McCormack, T., & Roessler, J. (Eds.). (2005). *Joint attention: Communication and other minds.* Oxford: Oxford University Press.

Morales, M., Mundy, P., Delgado, C. E. F., Yale, M., Messinger, D., Neal, R., *et al.* (2000). Responding to joint attention across the 6- through 24-month age period and early language acquisition. *Journal of Applied Developmental Psychology, 21*(3), 283–298.

Mundy, P., & Newell, L. (2007). Attention, joint attention, and social cognition. *Current Directions in Psychological Science, 16,* 269–274.

Schietecatte, I., Roeyers, H., & Warreyn, P. (2012). Exploring the nature of joint attention impairments in young children with autism spectrum disorder: Associated social and cognitive skills. *Journal of Autism and Developmental Disorders, 42*(1), 1–12.

Sensory Behaviors in Young Children with ASD

James, K., Miller, L. J., Schaaf, R., Nielsen, D. M., & Schoen, S. A. (2011). Phenotypes within sensory modulation dysfunction. *Comprehensive Psychiatry, 52*(6), 715–724.

Marco, E. J., Hinkley, L. B. N., Hill, S. S., & Nagarajan, S. S. (2011). Sensory processing in autism: A review of neurophysiologic findings. *Pediatric Research, 69,* 48–54.

Nadon, G., Ehrmann, D. F., Dunn, W. D., & Gisel, E. (2011). Association of sensory processing and eating problems in children with autism spectrum disorders. *Autism Research and Treatment.* doi:10.1155/2011/541926

Schaaf, R., & Blanche, E. I. (2011). Comparison of behavioral intervention and sensory-integration therapy in the treatment of challenging behavior. *Journal of Autism and Developmental Disorders, 41*(10), 1436–1438.

Schaaf, R. C., Toth-Cohen, S., Johnson, S. L., Outten, G., & Benevides, T. W. (2011). The everyday routines of families of children with autism: Examining the impact of sensory processing difficulties on the family. *Autism, 15*(3), 373–389.

Stephenson, J., & Carter, M. (2009). The use of weighted vests with children with autism spectrum disorders and other disabilities. *Journal of Autism and Developmental Disorders, 39*(1), 105–114.

Subject Index

Author Index